BELIEVE
DARE TO BELIEVE GOD AGAIN

Stacey Walker

Dedicated to
My wife Kori, my children Victoria, Stacie, Zavone, Nathan,
Ramon, and Monique, my grandchildren, my Freedom Church
family, and all the people who desire to have an intimate
relationship with God through the saving grace of Jesus Christ.
You are always in my heart and in my mind. May God always
keep you and give you good success.

Foreword

Stacey Walker came to help us at The Church at Hillsboro in Hillsboro, Missouri, after our pastor unexpectedly passed away. He stayed with my husband and I and became like a son to us. Eventually, he became the pastor of our church. Stacey is a man after God's own heart (Acts 13:22). One of his favorite scriptures is "Seek ye first the Kingdom of God and his righteousness and all these things shall be added unto you" (Matthew 6:33). He is a man who has applied the principles of God to his own life and grew in his walk with the Lord right before our eyes. He is an example of God's blessings in all areas of his life. His desire is to teach others how to do the same. This book covers all kinds of situations and shows you where to find the scriptures. I believe this book will help many people no matter where they are in their walk with the Lord.

Dear Friend and Spiritual mother,

Jeannie Hergenroeder

Preface

Resist the devil, and he will flee from you. Draw close to God, and He will draw near to you. This one thing is for sure: God is not a man that He should lie to you. All of His promises are yes and amen. God cannot and will not fail. Failure is not in Him, and neither is deception His way. This book, and every word in it, are written under the divine instruction and inspiration of the Holy Spirit. Is there anything too hard for God? He is the only God who knows and can secure your future. His plans for you are to give you the blessed and eternal hope in Jesus Christ and all the glorious benefits of the kingdom of God that come with it, now and forevermore.

Amen.

Introduction

This book is intended only to be a quick reference guide for appropriating the promises of God for any situation that you may have or be going through. What this book is not for is replacing your Bible or any other quality time that you may already spend with our heavenly Father. Now if you happen to be a non-believer who by some divine act of God has come across this book, it is my hope that the God of peace would move in your heart through the Holy Spirit to receive God's most precious gift to mankind. The gift I speak of is His only begotten Son and Savior of the world, Jesus Christ, who was crucified for our sins, died, and whom God raised from the grave so that whoever believed Him as God's saving grace would not perish but would receive everlasting life. So, my prayer is that this book will have a heartfelt impact on your life and would cause you to believe in God and accept Jesus Christ as your personal Lord and Savior, or at the very least make you curious enough to want to know more about Him and how much He loves you. Last, but not least, to those who may be prodigal sons or daughters who wish to return to the Lord, just simply come back. It's as easy as that! In any case, this book is designed to make you take immediate action. Now...

Dare to Believe God Again.

Next Step

Amplified Bible, Classic Edition, Acts 2:38

And Peter answered them, Repent (change your views and purpose to accept the will of God in your inner selves instead of rejecting it) and be baptized, every one of you, in the name of Jesus Christ for the forgiveness of and release from your sins; and you shall receive the gift of the Holy Spirit.

A WISE MAN SAID:

"Don't be afraid to start over again. This time, you're not starting from scratch, you're starting from experience."

Invitation

Heavenly Father,

I do believe, with all of my heart and soul, you love me.

I believe that you sent your only Son, Jesus Christ, to die for me.

I believe He died, was buried, and was raised to life again by your awe-inspiring power and love.

I also believe that He sits at your right hand, and you have placed all power and authority in His hands.

I accept that by accepting Jesus, all my sins will be forgiven, and I will be given the eternal love, life, and land of the Father.

I gladly open my heart to receive Jesus Christ as my Lord, Savior, and King. Father, I thank you for entering my heart— because with all my heart, I truly believe.

Amen

CHAPTER ONE

Who Is God To You?

To answer your question of who God is to you, let us establish who He is not. God is not a figure of our imagination. He is as real as the fingers on your hand. He's not some ancient mythological old man in a white robe with white hair peering at us from behind a cloud. God is not like some tyrant ready to cast hell and damnation upon anyone who disagrees with Him. Nor is He a collection of fabricated stories or excuses to make us feel better because one cannot seem to handle life and all of its twists and turns. So, this brings us back to the original question, who is God to you? Well, it has been said that "if you really want to know something about a person, ask them for yourself." And yes, by the way, God is a person. In the first chapter, we will let God speak for Himself in His own Word. This will take the guesswork out of your mind about who He is or who He is to you. As you read through each verse, ask God to speak to your heart.

Now, I will heat up my coffee while God and you get to know each other or get reacquainted through the next page or two. Let's all meet again in chapter two.

In the beginning, God (prepared, formed, fashioned, and) created the heavens and the earth (AMP, Genesis 1:1).

In all of your troubles, you may finally decide that you want to worship only the Lord. And if you turn back to him and obey him completely, he will again be your God (CEV, Deuteronomy 4:29-30).

Understand, therefore, that the Lord your God is the faithful God who for a thousand generations keeps his promises and constantly loves those who love him and who obey his commands (TLB, Deuteronomy 7:9).

The Lord is a mighty rock, and he never does wrong. God can always be trusted to bring justice (CEV, Deuteronomy 32:4).

Wherefore thou art great, O Jehovah God: for there is none like thee, neither is there any God besides thee, according to all that we have heard with our ears (ASV, 2 Samuel 7:22).

O taste and see that the Lord is good; blessed is the man that trusteth in Him! (KJ21, Psalms 34:8).

I have been young and now I am old. And in all my years, I have never seen the Lord forsake a man who loves him; nor have I seen the children of the godly go hungry (TLB, Psalms 37:25).

"I am God—yes, I Am. I haven't changed. And because I haven't changed, you, the descendants of Jacob, haven't been destroyed. You have a long history of ignoring my commands. You haven't done a thing I've told you. Return to me so I can return to you," says God-of-the-Angel-Armies. "You ask, 'But how do we return?'" (MSG, Malachi 3:6-7).

For God so greatly loved and dearly prized the world that He [even] gave up His only begotten (unique) Son, so that whoever believes in (trusts in, clings to, relies on) Him shall not perish (come to destruction, be lost) but have eternal (everlasting) life (AMP, John 3:16).

God is spirit, and it is necessary to worship God in spirit and truth (CEB, John 4:24).

Peter said, "Change your life. Turn to God and be baptized, each of you, in the name of Jesus Christ, so your sins are forgiven. Receive the gift of the Holy Spirit. The promise is targeted to you and your children, but also to all who are far away —whomever, in fact, our Master God invites" (MSG, Acts 2:38-39).

So, my very dear friends, don't get thrown off course. Every desirable and beneficial gift comes out of heaven. The gifts are rivers of light cascading down from the Father of Light. There is nothing deceitful in God, nothing two-faced, nothing fickle. He brought us to life using the true Word, showing us off as the crown of all his creatures (MSG, James 1:17-18).

The person who doesn't love does not know God, because God is love (CEB, 1 John 4:8).

So you see, our love for him comes as a result of his loving us first (TLB, 1 John 4:19).

I am the Alpha and the Omega, the First and the Last (the Before all and the End of all) (AMP, Revelation 22:13).

CHAPTER TWO

You Are More Than Just a Servant to God, You Are a Son

Welcome back. I hope you had a delightful time engaging with the Word of God and learning His true identity. The relationship you share with God is essential for spiritual growth and quality of life. It should be just as important to you as it is to Him. Don't you know that you are more than just God's creation? If you have believed in and received Jesus Christ into your life, you are not just a mere servant of God, but a son. The word "son" in this text includes both male and female gender and identifies you as a spiritual offspring—a unique people not of human birth, but a rebirth, born of the spirit. In this chapter, let us look at the rights and privileges of our sonship. And always remember, "We are not sons because we serve; we serve because we are sons."

I will tell the promise that the Lord made to me: "You are my son, because today I have become your father" (Psalms 2:7, CEV).

But his father said to the slaves, "Quick! Bring the finest robe in the house and put it on him. And a jeweled ring for his finger; and shoes! And kill the calf we have in the fattening pen. We must celebrate with a feast, for this son of mine was dead and has returned to life. He was lost and is found." So, the party began (TLB, Luke 15:11-32).

But as many as received Him, to them gave He the power to become the sons of God, even to those who believe in His name (KJ21, John 1:12).

The Spirit Himself testifies with our spirit that we are children of God (NIV, Romans 8:16).

And the heathen, of whom it once was said, "You are not my people," shall be called "sons of the Living God" (TLB, Romans 9:26)

"And I will be a father to you, and you shall be sons and daughters to Me," says the Lord Almighty (NLT, 2 Corinthians 6:18).

Now we are no longer slaves but God's own sons. And since we are his sons, everything he has belongs to us, for that is the way God planned (TLB, Galatians 4:7).

CHAPTER THREE
The Others

How and why do others matter when it comes to God blessing me?

The world we live in has become more and more absorbed with self. We hear it advertised 24 hours a day, 7 days a week. Our eyes and ears are flooded with the propaganda of me, myself, and I. We hear and see it in songs, movies, advertisements, etc. God does not want us to become desensitized when it comes to others. Our blessings and the promises of God all revolve around how we treat each other, and we're all part of the same family — the human race. How can you seriously believe that God would do things for you when you don't care about others? In order to get the waterfall of God's blessings flowing in your life, one of the first things you must do is learn to do good to others.

Quotes

"The greatest blessing in the whole world is being a blessing."

— Jack Hyles

"When God blesses you financially, don't raise your standard of living. Raise your standard of giving."

— Mark Batterson

"God didn't add another day to your life because you needed it. He did it because someone out there needs you!"

— Amy Martin-Vargas

"A kind gesture can reach a wound that only compassion can heal."

— Steve Maraboli

Doing good does not come automatically. We can start by reading and practicing daily the scriptures that are found below.

If you give to others, you will be given a full amount in return. It will be packed down, shaken together, and spilling over into your lap. The way you treat others is the way you will be treated (CEV, Luke 6:38).

My command is this: Love each other as I have loved you (NIV, John 15:12).

And do not forget to do good and to share with others, for with such sacrifices, God is pleased (NIV, Hebrews 13:16).

CHAPTER FOUR

A Band of Brothers

Through every pain	*Stand firm in the faith*
God is there, though it seems.	*and*
He doesn't care.	*only believe.*
When condolences	*the rain will cease,*
and such	*and the*
Just won't do, and	*Son will shine*
it takes	*and those*
much more to get	*Band of Brothers*
you through,	*Loss, Hurt, and Pain*
the pain, hurt, or loss that	*left far behind.*
you've conceived.	

God takes no pleasure in seeing anyone suffer.

God is close to the broken-hearted. He is the physician of healing, hurt, and pain. He will cross the rugged terrains of the world to retrieve our lost possessions for us. He lovingly seeks out those who have lost their way in life. God wants you to let Him know about all your concerns because He cares for you. For Him, there is no problem too great or none too small to handle. We all have undoubtedly suffered loss, hurt, or pain of some kind and for some, to the point that there seems to be no way of getting through it. God does not want to minimize anyone's grief because, in the person of Jesus Christ, Christ himself knew many sorrows. Sadly, there is no avoiding the problems of this life, but joyfully, by His powerful life-changing gentle spirit, He desires to accompany us through them all. So, by the Words of the only true and awesome God that are within the next few pages of this chapter, find your comfort, find your peace, and with God's guidance you can continually navigate your way through the valley of loss, hurt, and pain.

(All citations ESV unless otherwise noted)

Have I not commanded you? Be strong and courageous. Do not be frightened, and do not be dismayed, for the Lord your God is with you wherever you go (Joshua 1:9).

This would be my comfort; I would even exult in pain unsparing, for I have not denied the words of the Holy One (Job, 6:10).

The Lord is a stronghold for the oppressed, a stronghold in times of trouble (Psalms 9:9).

The Lord is my rock and my fortress and my deliverer, my God, my rock, in whom I take refuge, my shield, and the horn of my salvation, my stronghold (Psalms 18:2).

Let the words of my mouth and the meditation of my heart be acceptable in your sight, O Lord, my rock and my redeemer (Psalms 19:14).

For he has not despised or abhorred the affliction of the afflicted, and he has not hidden his face from him but has heard when he cried to him (Psalms 22:24).

One thing have I asked of the Lord, that will I seek after: that I may dwell in the house of the Lord all the days of my life, to gaze upon the beauty of the Lord and to inquire in his temple. For he will hide me in his shelter in the day of trouble; he will conceal me under the cover of his tent; he will lift me high upon a rock (Psalms 27:4-5).

Wait for the Lord; be strong, and let your heart take courage; wait for the Lord! (Psalms 27:14).

His anger lasts a moment; his favor lasts for life! Weeping may go on all night, but in the morning there is joy (TLB, Psalms 30:5).

God is our refuge and strength, a very present help in trouble. Therefore, we will not fear though the earth gives way, though the mountains be moved into the heart of the sea, though its waters roar and foam, though the mountains tremble at its swelling. Selah There is a river whose streams make glad the city of God, the holy habitation of the Most High. God is in the midst of her; she shall not be moved; God will help her when morning dawns (Psalms 46:1-5).

You have kept count of my tossing's; put my tears in your bottle. Are they not in your book? (Psalms 56:8).

You who have made me see many troubles and calamities will revive me again; from the depths of the earth, you will bring me up again. You will increase my greatness and comfort me again (Psalms 71:20-21).

Truly God is good to Israel, to those who are pure in heart. But as for me, my feet had almost stumbled, my steps had nearly slipped. For I was envious of the arrogant when I saw the prosperity of the wicked. For they have no pangs until death; their bodies are fat and sleek. They are not in trouble as others are; they are not stricken like the rest of mankind (Psalms 73:1-5).

He who dwells in the shelter of the Most High will abide in the shadow of the Almighty. I will say to the Lord, "My refuge and my fortress, my God, in whom I trust." For he will deliver you from the snare of the fowler and from the deadly pestilence. He will cover you with his pinions, and under his wings you will find refuge; his faithfulness is a shield and buckler. You will not fear the terror of the night, nor the arrow that flies by day (Psalms

91:1-5).

I love the Lord, because he has heard my voice and my pleas for mercy. Because he inclined his ear to me, therefore I will call on him as long as I live (Psalms 116:1-2).

Let your steadfast love comfort me according to your promise to your servant (Psalms 119:76).

Though I walk in the midst of trouble, you preserve my life; you stretch out your hand against the wrath of my enemies, and your right hand delivers me (Psalms 138:7).

He heals the brokenhearted and binds up their wounds (Psalms 147:3).

Trust in the Lord with all your heart, and do not lean on your own understanding (Proverbs 3:5).

A friend loves at all times, and a brother is born for adversity (Proverbs 17:17).

For I know the plans I have for you, declares the Lord, plans for welfare and not for evil, to give you a future and hope (Jeremiah 29:11).

He will swallow up death forever, and the Lord God will wipe away tears from all faces, and the reproach of his people he will take away from all the earth, for the Lord has spoken (Isaiah 25:8).

He was despised and rejected by men; a man of sorrows and acquainted with grief; and as one from whom men hide their faces he was despised, and we esteemed him not. Surely, he has borne our griefs and carried our sorrows; yet we esteemed him stricken, smitten by God, and afflicted. But he was wounded for our transgressions; he was crushed for our iniquities; upon him was the chastisement that brought us peace, and with his stripes, we are healed (Isaiah 53:3-5).

For the Lord will not cast off forever, but, though he causes grief, he will have compassion according to the abundance of his steadfast love; for he does not willingly afflict or grieve the children of men (Lamentations 3:31-33).

The Lord your God is in your midst, a mighty one who will save; he will rejoice over you with gladness; he will quiet you by his love; he will exult over you with loud singing (Zephaniah 3:17).

Blessed are those who mourn, for they shall be comforted (Matthew 5:4).

But I say to you that everyone who is angry with his brother will be liable to judgment; whoever insults his brother will be liable to the council; and whoever says, 'You fool!' will be liable to the hell of fire (Matthew 5:22).

Do not be like them, for your Father knows what you need before you ask him (Matthew 6:8).

Therefore, I tell you, do not be anxious about your life, what you will eat or what you will drink, nor about your body, what you will put on. Is not life more than food, and the body more than clothing? Look at the birds of the air: they neither sow nor reap nor gather into barns, and yet your heavenly Father feeds them. Are you not of more value than they? And which of you by being anxious can add a single hour to his span of life? And why are you anxious about clothing? Consider the lilies of the field, how they grow: they neither toil nor spin, yet I tell you, even Solomon in all his glory was not arrayed like one of these (Matthew 6:25-29).

Come to me, all who labor and are heavy laden, and I will give you rest. Take my yoke upon you, and learn from me, for I am gentle and lowly in heart, and you will find rest for your souls. For my yoke is easy, and my burden is light (Matthew 11:28-30).

For God so loved the world, that he gave his only Son, that whoever believes in him should not perish but have eternal life. For God did not send his Son into the world to condemn the world, but in order that the world might be saved through him (John 3:16-17).

Jesus answered, "It was not that this man sinned, or his parents, but that the works of God might be displayed in him" (John 9:3).

"Let not your hearts be troubled. Believe in God; believe also in me. In my Father's house are many rooms. If it were not so, would I have told you that I go to prepare a place for you? And if I go and prepare a place for you, I will come again and will take you to myself, that where I am you may be also" (John 14:1-3).

Peace, I leave with you; my peace I give to you. Not as the world gives do I give to you. Let not your hearts be troubled, neither let them be afraid (John 14:27).

So also, you have sorrow now, but I will see you again, and your hearts will rejoice, and no one will take your joy from you (John 16:22).

I have said these things to you, that in me you may have peace. In the world you will have tribulation. But take heart; I have overcome the world (John 16:33).

More than that, we rejoice in our sufferings, knowing that suffering produces endurance, and endurance produces character, and character produces hope, and hope does not put us to shame, because God's love has been poured into our hearts through the Holy Spirit who has been given to us (Romans 5:3-5).

For I consider that the sufferings of this present time are not worth comparing with the glory that is to be revealed to us (Romans 8:18).

For we know that the whole creation has been groaning together in the pains of childbirth until now (Romans 8:22).

Bless those who persecute you; bless and do not curse them (Romans 12:14).

Beloved, never avenge yourselves, but leave it to the wrath of God, for it is written, "Vengeance is mine, I will repay, says the Lord" (Romans 12:19).

Do not be overcome by evil but overcome evil with good (Romans 12:21).

May the God of hope fill you with all joy and peace in believing, so that by the power of the Holy Spirit you may abound in hope (Romans 15:13).

And we know that for those who love God all things work together for good, for those who are called according to his purpose (Romans 8:28).

No temptation has overtaken you that is not common to man. God is faithful, and he will not let you be tempted beyond your ability, but with the temptation he will also provide the way of escape, that you may be able to endure it (1 Corinthians 10:13).

For God is not a God of confusion but of peace. As in all the churches of the saints (1 Corinthians 14:33).

So, we do not lose heart. Though our outer self is wasting away, our inner self is being renewed day by day. For this light momentary affliction is preparing for us an eternal weight of glory beyond all comparison, as we look not to the things that are seen but to the things that are unseen. For the things that are seen are transient, but the things that are unseen are eternal (2 Corinthians 4:16-18).

As it is, I rejoice, not because you were grieved, but because you were grieved into repenting. For you felt a godly grief, so that you suffered no loss through us (2 Corinthians 7:9).

But he said to me, "My grace is sufficient for you, for my power is made perfect in weakness." Therefore, I will boast all the more gladly of my weaknesses, so that the power of Christ may rest upon me. For the sake of Christ, then, I am content with weaknesses, insults, hardships, persecutions, and calamities. For when I am weak, then I am strong (2 Corinthians 12:9-10).

Be kind to one another, tenderhearted, forgiving one another, as God in Christ forgave you (Ephesians 4:32).

Do not be anxious about anything, but in everything by prayer and supplication with thanksgiving let your requests be made known to God. And the peace of God, which surpasses all understanding, will guard your hearts and your minds in Christ Jesus (Philippians 4:6-7).

I can do all things through him who strengthens me (Philippians

4:13).

Bearing with one another and, if one has a complaint against another, forgiving each other; as the Lord has forgiven you, so you also must forgive (Colossians 3:13).

But we do not want you to be uninformed, brothers, about those who are asleep, that you may not grieve as others do who have no hope. For since we believe that Jesus died and rose again, even so, through Jesus, God will bring with him those who have fallen asleep. For this we declare to you by a word from the Lord, that we who are alive, who are left until the coming of the Lord, will not precede those who have fallen asleep. For the Lord himself will descend from heaven with a cry of command, with the voice of an archangel, and with the sound of the trumpet of God. And the dead in Christ will rise first. Then we who are alive, who are left, will be caught up together with them in the clouds to meet the Lord in the air, and so we will always be with the Lord. Therefore encourage one another with those words (1 Thessalonians 4:13-18).

Let no one despise you for your youth, but set the believers an example in speech, in conduct, in love, in faith, in purity (1 Timothy 4:12).

Indeed, all who desire to live a godly life in Christ Jesus will be persecuted (2 Timothy 3:12).

For because he himself has suffered when tempted, he is able to help those who are being tempted (Hebrews 2:18).

For we do not have a high priest who is unable to sympathize with our weaknesses, but one who in every respect has been tempted as we are, yet without sin. Let us then with confidence draw near to the throne of grace, that we may receive mercy and find grace to help in time of need (Hebrews 4:15-16).

And just as it is appointed for man to die once, and after that comes judgment (Hebrews 9:27).

And have you forgotten the exhortation that addresses you as sons? "My son do not regard lightly the discipline of the Lord, nor be weary when reproved by him. For the Lord disciplines the one he loves and chastises every son whom he receives." It is for discipline that you have to endure. God is treating you as sons. For what son is there whom his father does not discipline? (Hebrews 12:5-7).

Keep your life free from love of money, and be content with what you have, for he has said, "I will never leave you nor forsake you" (Hebrews 13:5).

Count it all joy, my brothers, when you meet trials of various kinds, for you know that the testing of your faith produces steadfastness. And let steadfastness have its full effect, that you may be perfect and complete, lacking in nothing (James 1:2-4).

For this is a gracious thing, when, mindful of God, one endures sorrows while suffering unjustly (1 Peter 2:19).

For it is better to suffer for doing good, if that should be God's will, than for doing evil. For Christ also suffered once for sins, the righteous for the unrighteous, that he might bring us to God, being put to death in the flesh but made alive in the spirit (1 Peter 3:17-18).

Beloved, do not be surprised at the fiery trial when it comes upon you to test you, as though something strange were happening to you. But rejoice insofar as you share Christ's sufferings, that you may also rejoice and be glad when his glory is revealed (1 Peter 4:12-13).

Therefore, let those who suffer according to God's will entrust their souls to a faithful Creator while doing good (1 Peter 4:19).

Humble yourselves, therefore, under the mighty hand of God so that at the proper time he may exalt you, casting all your anxieties on him, because he cares for you (1 Peter 5:6-7).

Do not fear what you are about to suffer. Behold, the devil is about to throw some of you into prison, that you may be tested, and for ten days you will have tribulation. Be faithful unto death, and I will give you the crown of life (Revelation 2:10).

He will wipe away every tear from their eyes, and death shall be no more, neither shall there be mourning, nor crying, nor pain anymore, for the former things have passed away (Revelation 21:4).

CHAPTER FIVE

Can You Hear Me Now? (Does God Really Hear Our Prayers?)

"Clearing out hindrances in our lives will enable us to live in harmony with God and others and have confidence in prayer."

— Dr. Myles Munroe

"The one prayer God always hears is the prayer of salvation through Jesus Christ."

— Pastor Terrell Somerville

If you have not made Jesus Christ Lord and Savior of your life, I urge you at this point to **STOP** reading. Go back to the beginning of this book to the next steps and invite Jesus into your life today.

The Bible says God's answers to prayer are yes and amen. However, we know some prayers are not answered. If you've ever wondered why or been confused, you're not alone. One sure way to clear this up is to see what the Bible says are some possible things that may cause our prayers to not be heard. God is not hard of hearing, neither is He deaf. So, if that is the case, then we must not be speaking His language. God's language is and has always been His word. Reading and studying His word teaches us how to pray and correctly communicate with God.

All Scripture is God-breathed and is useful for teaching, rebuking, correcting, and training in righteousness (2 Timothy 3:16).

The man who turns away from the truth lest he should get to know it will not receive answers to prayer (Proverbs 28:9).

If you find your prayers are not being answered, review and reflect on the following 27 possible reasons for unanswered prayers.

27 POSSIBLE REASONS FOR UNANSWERED PRAYER
(All citations CEV unless otherwise noted)

1. Refusing to hear the truth.
   God cannot stand the prayers of anyone who disobeys his Law (Proverbs 28:9).

2. Tempting or provoking God.
   But the Lord was angry with me because of you people, and he refused to listen. "That's enough!" he said. "I don't want to hear any more" (Deuteronomy 3:26).

3. Lack of charity or love for others.
   If you won't help the poor, don't expect to be heard when you cry out for help (Proverbs 21:13).

4. Lack of humility.
   If my own people will humbly pray and turn back to me and stop sinning, then I will answer them from heaven. I will forgive them and make their land fertile once again (2 Chronicles 7:14).

5. A hardened heart.
   But everyone who heard those prophets stubbornly refused to obey. Instead, they turned their backs on everything my Spirit had commanded the earlier prophets to preach. So, I, the Lord, became angry (Zechariah 7:12, 13).

6. Forsaking God.
   At once, Azariah went to Asa and said: Listen to me, King Asa and you people of Judah and Benjamin. The Lord will be with you and help you, as long as you obey and worship him. But if you disobey him, he will desert you (2 Chronicles 15:2).

7. Praying amiss (wrong motives).

Yet even when you do pray, your prayers are not answered, because you pray just for selfish reasons (James 4:3).

8. Regarding iniquity.

If my thoughts had been sinful, he would have refused to hear me (Psalms 66:18).

9. Unbelief.

Jesus replied: It is because you don't have enough faith! But I can promise you this. If you had faith no larger than a mustard seed, you could tell this mountain to move from here to there. And it would. Everything would be possible for you (Matthew 17:20,21; Matthew 21:22).

10. Marital strife.

If you are a husband, you should be thoughtful of your wife. Treat her with honor, because she isn't as strong as you are, and she shares with you in the gift of life. Then nothing will stand in the way of your prayers (1 Peter 3:7).

11. Parading your prayer-life.

God blesses those people who want to obey him more than to eat or drink. They will be given what they want! (Matthew 5:6).

12. Sin.

Why do you fight and argue with each other? Isn't it because you are full of selfish desires that fight to control your body? You want something you don't have, and you will do anything to get it. You will even kill! But you still cannot get what you want, and you won't get it by fighting and arguing. You should pray for it. Yet even when you do pray, your prayers are not answered, because you pray just for selfish reasons. You people aren't faithful to God! Don't you know if you love the world, you are

God's enemies? And if you decide to be a friend of the world, you make yourself an enemy of God. Do you doubt the Scriptures that say, "God truly cares about the Spirit he has put in us?" (James 4:1-5; Isaiah 59:2; John 9:31).

Your sins are the roadblock between you and your God. That's why he doesn't answer your prayers or let you see his face (Isaiah 59:2).

We know that God listens only to people who love and obey him. God doesn't listen to sinners (John 9:31).

13. Vain (useless) repetitions.

When you pray, don't talk on and on as people do who don't know God. They think God likes to hear long prayers (Matthew 6:7).

14. Being discouraged.

Jesus told his disciples a story about how they should keep on praying and never give up: In a town there was once a judge who didn't fear God or care about people. In that same town there was a widow who kept going to the judge and saying, "Make sure that I get fair treatment in court." For a while the judge refused to do anything. Finally, he said to himself, "Even though I don't fear God or care about people, I will help this widow because she keeps on bothering me. If I don't help her, she will wear me out." The Lord said: Think about what that crooked judge said. Won't God protect his chosen ones who pray to him day and night? Won't he be concerned for them? He will surely hurry and help them. But when the Son of Man comes, will he find on this earth anyone with faith? (Luke 18:1-8).

15. Doubt and double-mindedness.

If any of you need wisdom, you should ask God, and it will be given to you. God is generous and won't correct you for asking. But when you ask for something, you must have faith and not doubt. Anyone who doubts is like an ocean wave tossed around in a storm. If you are that kind of person, you can't make up your mind, and you surely can't be trusted. So don't expect the Lord to give you anything at all (James 1:5-8).

16. Anxiety and worry.

Don't worry about anything but pray about everything. With thankful hearts, offer up your prayers and requests to God (Philippians 4:6).

17. Hypocrisy.

Jesus told a story to some people who thought they were better than others and who looked down on everyone else: Two men went into the temple to pray. One was a Pharisee and the other a tax collector. The Pharisee stood over by himself and prayed, "God, I thank you that I am not greedy, dishonest, and unfaithful in marriage like other people. And I am really glad that I am not like that tax collector over there. I go without eating for two days a week, and I give you one tenth of all I earn." The tax collector stood off at a distance and did not think he was good enough even to look up toward heaven. He was so sorry for what he had done that he pounded his chest and prayed, "God, have pity on me! I am such a sinner." Then Jesus said, "When the two men went home, it was the tax collector and not the Pharisee who was pleasing to God. If you put yourself above others, you will be put down. But if you humble yourself, you will be honored" (Luke 18:9-14).

18. Unforgiveness.

If you forgive others for the wrongs they do to you, your Father in heaven will forgive you. But if you don't forgive others, your Father will not forgive your sins. Whenever you stand up to pray, you must forgive what others have done to you. Then your Father in heaven will forgive your sins (Matthew 6:14, 15; Mark 11:25, 26).

19. Not tithing.

You people are robbing me, your God. And, here you are, asking, "How are we robbing you?" You are robbing me of the offerings and of the ten percent that belongs to me. That's why your whole nation is under a curse. I am the Lord All-Powerful, and I challenge you to put me to the test. Bring the entire ten percent into the storehouse, so there will be food in my house. Then I will open the windows of heaven and flood you with blessing after blessing (Malachi 3:8,9,10).

20. Rebellion against God's Word.

You completely ignored me and refused to listen. You rejected my advice and paid no attention when I warned you. So, when you are struck by some terrible disaster, or when trouble and distress surround you like a whirlwind, I will laugh and make fun. You will ask for my help, but I won't listen. You will search, but you won't find me.

But everyone who heard those prophets stubbornly refused to obey. Instead, they turned their backs on everything my Spirit had commanded the earlier prophets to preach. So, I, the Lord, became angry and said, "You people paid no attention when I called out to you, and now I'll pay no attention when you call out to me." That's why I came with a whirlwind and scattered them among foreign nations, leaving their lovely country empty of people and in ruins (Proverbs 1:24-28; Zechariah 7:11-14).

21. Presumption and pride.

Two men went into the temple to pray. One was a Pharisee and the other a tax collector. The Pharisee stood over by himself and prayed, "God, I thank you that I am not greedy, dishonest, and unfaithful in marriage like other people. And I am really glad that I am not like that tax collector over there. I go without eating for two days a week, and I give you one tenth of all I earn." The tax collector stood off at a distance and did not think he was good enough even to look up toward heaven. He was so sorry for what he had done that he pounded his chest and prayed, "God, have pity on me! I am such a sinner." Then Jesus said, "When the two men went home, it was the tax collector and not the Pharisee who was pleasing to God. If you put yourself above others, you will be put down. But if you humble yourself, you will be honored (Luke 18:10-14).

22. Unconfessed sin.

If my thoughts had been sinful, he would have refused to hear me (Psalms 66:18).

23. Demonic attack.

Then he said, "Don't be frightened, Daniel, for your request has been heard in heaven and was answered the very first day you began to fast before the Lord and pray for understanding; that very day I was sent here to meet you. But for twenty-one days, the mighty Evil Spirit who overrules the kingdom of Persia blocked my way. Then Michael, one of the top officers of the heavenly army, came to help me, so that I was able to break through these spirit rulers of Persia. Now I am here to tell you what will happen to your people, the Jews, at the end times—for the fulfillment of this prophecy is many years away" (TLB, Daniel 10:12-14).

24. Lack of sincerity.

When you pray, don't be like those show-offs who love to stand up and pray in the synagogues and on the street corners. They do this just to look good. I can assure you that they already have their reward (Matthew 6:5).

25. Being unsaved (an unbeliever).

After Jesus had finished speaking to his disciples, he looked up toward heaven and prayed: Father, the time has come for you to bring glory to your Son, in order that he may bring glory to you. And you gave him power over all people, so he would give eternal life to everyone you give him. Eternal life is to know you, the only true God, and to know Jesus Christ, the one you sent. I have brought glory to you here on earth by doing everything you gave me to do. Now, Father, give me back the glory I had with you before the world was created. You have given me some followers from this world, and I have shown them what you are like. They were yours, but you gave them to me, and they have obeyed you. They know that you gave me everything I have. I told my followers what you told me, and they accepted it. They know I came from you, and they believe you are the one who sent me. I am praying for them, but not for those who belong to this world. My followers belong to you, and I am praying for them. All I have is yours, and all you have is mine, and they will bring glory to me. Holy Father, I am no longer in the world. I am coming to you, but my followers are still in the world. So, keep them safe by the power of the name you have given me. Then they will be one with each other, just as you and I are one. While I was with them, I kept them safe by the power you have given me. I guarded them, and not one of them was lost, except the one who had to be lost. This happened so that what the Scriptures say would come true. I am on my way to you. But I say these things while I am still in the world, so my followers will have the same complete joy that I do. I have told them your message. But the people of this world hate them, because they don't belong to this world, just as I don't. Father, I don't ask you to take my followers out of the world, but keep them safe from the evil one. They don't belong to this world, and neither do I. Your word is the truth. So let this truth make them completely yours. I am sending them into the world, just as you sent me. I have given myself completely for their sake, so they may belong completely to the truth. I am not praying just for these followers. I am also praying for everyone else who will have faith because of what my followers will say about me. I want all of them to be one with each other, just as I am one with you and you are one with me. I also want them to be one with us. Then the people of this world will believe that you sent me. I have honored my followers in the same way you honored me, in order that they may be one with each other, just as we are one. I am one with them, and you are one with me, so they may become completely one. Then this world's people will know that you sent me. They will know that you love my followers as much as you love me. Father, I want everyone you have given me to be with me, wherever I am. Then they will see the glory you have given me, because you loved me before the world was created. Good Father, the people of this world don't know you. But I know you, and my followers know that you sent me. I told them what you are like, and I will tell them even more. Then the love you have for me will become part of them, and I will be one with them (John 17).

26. Curses.

The Lord Will Bless You if You Obey. Moses said to Israel:

Today I am giving you the laws and teachings of the Lord your God. Always obey them, and the Lord will make Israel the most famous and important nation on earth, and he will bless you in many ways. The Lord will make your businesses and your farms successful. You will have many children. You will harvest large crops, and your herds of cattle and flocks of sheep and goats will produce many young. You will have plenty of bread to eat. The Lord will make you successful in your daily work. The Lord will help you defeat your enemies and make them scatter in all directions. The Lord your God is giving you the land, and he will make sure you are successful in everything you do. Your harvests will be so large that your storehouses will be full. If you follow and obey the Lord, he will make you his own special people, just as he promised. Then everyone on earth will know that you belong to the Lord, and they will be afraid of you. The Lord will give you a lot of children and make sure that your animals give birth to many young. The Lord promised your ancestors that this land would be yours, and he will make it produce large crops for you. The Lord will open the storehouses of the skies where he keeps the rain, and he will send rain on your land at just the right times. He will make you successful in everything you do. You will have plenty of money to lend to other nations, but you won't need to borrow any yourself. Obey the laws and teachings that I'm giving you today, and the Lord your God will make Israel a leader among the nations, and not a follower. Israel will be wealthy and powerful, not poor and weak. But you must not reject any of his laws and teachings or worship other gods (Deuteronomy 28).

The Lord Will Put Curses on You if You Disobey. Moses said:

Israel, today I am giving you the laws and teachings of the Lord your God. And if you don't obey them all, he will put many curses on you. Your businesses and farms will fail. You won't have enough bread to eat. You'll have only a few children, your crops will be small, and your herds of cattle and flocks of sheep and goats won't produce many young. The Lord will make you fail in everything you do. No matter what you try to accomplish, the Lord will confuse you, and you will feel his anger. You won't last long, and you may even meet with disaster, all because you rejected the Lord. The Lord will send terrible diseases to attack you, and you will never be well again. You will suffer with burning fever and swelling and pain until you die somewhere in the land that you captured. The Lord will make the sky overhead seem like a bronze roof that keeps out the rain, and the ground under your feet will become as hard as iron. Your crops will be scorched by the hot east wind or ruined by mildew. He will send dust and sandstorms instead of rain, and you will be wiped out. The Lord will let you be defeated by your enemies, and you will scatter in all directions. You will be a horrible sight for the other nations to see, and no one will disturb the birds and wild animals while they eat your dead bodies. The Lord will make you suffer with diseases that will cause oozing sores or crusty itchy patches on your skin or boils like the ones that are common in Egypt. And there will be no cure for you! You will become insane and go blind. The Lord will make you so confused, that even in bright sunshine you will have to feel your way around like a blind person, who cannot tell day from night. For the rest of your life, people will beat and rob you, and no one will be able to stop them. A man will be engaged to a woman, but before they can get married, she will be raped by enemy soldiers. Some of you will build houses, but never get to live in them. If you plant a vineyard, you won't be around long enough to enjoy the first harvest. Your cattle will be killed while you watch, but you won't get to eat any of the meat. Your donkeys and sheep will be stolen from you, and no one will be around to force your enemies to give them back. Your sons and daughters will be dragged off to a foreign country while you stand there helpless. And even if you watch for them until you go blind, you will never see them again. You will work hard on your farms, but everything you harvest will be eaten by foreigners, who will mistreat you and abuse you for the rest of your life. What you see will be so horrible that you will go insane and the Lord will punish you from head to toe with boils that never heal. The Lord will let you and your king be taken captive to a country that you and your ancestors have never even heard of, and there you will have to worship idols made of wood and stone. People of nearby countries will shudder when they see your terrible troubles, but they will still make fun of you. You will plant a lot of seed, but gather a small harvest, because locusts will eat your crops. You will plant vineyards and work hard at taking care of them, but you won't gather any grapes, much less get any wine, because the vines themselves will be eaten by worms. Even if your olive trees grow everywhere in your country, the olives will fall off before they are ready, and there won't be enough olive oil for combing your hair. Even your children will be taken as prisoners of war. Locusts will eat your crops and strip your trees of leaves and fruit. Foreigners in your towns will become wealthy and powerful, while you become poor and powerless. You will be so short of money that you will have to borrow from those foreigners. They will be the leaders in the community, and you will be the followers (Leviticus 26:15-46).

More Curses for Disobedience. Moses said:

Israel, if you don't obey the laws and teachings that the Lord your God is giving you, he will send these curses to chase, attack, and destroy you. Then everyone will look at you and your descendants and realize that the Lord has placed you under a curse. If the Lord makes you wealthy, but you don't joyfully worship and honor him, he will send enemies to attack you and make you their slaves. Then you will live in poverty with nothing to eat, drink, or wear, and your owners will work you to death. Foreigners who speak a strange language will be sent to attack you without warning, just like an eagle swooping down. They won't show any mercy, and they will have no respect for old people or pity for children. They will take your cattle, sheep, goats, grain, wine, and olive oil, then leave you to starve. All over the land that the Lord your God gave you, the enemy army will surround your towns. You may feel safe inside your town walls, but the enemy will tear them down while you wait in horror. Finally, you will get so hungry that you will eat the sons and daughters that the Lord gave you. Because of hunger, a man who had been gentle and kind will eat his own children and refuse to share the meal with his brother or wife or with his other children. A woman may have grown up in such luxury that she never had to put a foot on the ground. But times will be so bad that she will secretly eat both her newborn baby and the afterbirth, without sharing any with her husband or her other children.

Disobedience Brings Destruction. Moses said to Israel:

You must obey everything in The Book of God's Law. Because if you don't respect the Lord, he will punish you and your descendants with incurable diseases, like those you were so afraid of in Egypt. Remember! If the Lord decides to destroy your nation, he can use any disease or disaster, not just the ones written in The Book of God's Law. There are as many of you now as the stars in the sky, but if you disobey the Lord your God, only a few of you will be left. The Lord is happy to make you successful and to help your nation grow while you conquer the land. But if you disobey him, he will be just as happy to pull you up by your roots. Those of you that survive will be scattered to every nation on earth, and you will have to worship stone and wood idols that never helped you or your ancestors. You will be restless—always longing for home, but never able to return. You will live in constant fear of death. Each morning you will wake up to such terrible sights that you will say, "I wish it were night!" But at night you will be terrified and say, "I wish it were day!" I told you never to go back to Egypt. But now the Lord himself will load you on ships and send you back. Then you will even try to sell yourselves as slaves, but no one will be interested.

27. Willful stubbornness.

And you have done even worse! You are stubborn, and instead of obeying me, you do whatever evil comes to your mind (Jeremiah 16:12,13).

CHAPTER SIX

No Worries

The seeds that fell among the thornbushes are also people who hear the message. But they start worrying about the needs of this life and are fooled by the desire to get rich. So, the message gets choked out, and they never produce anything (CEV, Matthew 13:22).

In this life, anything that can happen will happen. So don't be surprised when the utility bills come faster than expected. Believe it or not, they came at the same time last month. The car won't start, she nags too much, he never listens to me, the kids are not behaving, and on top of that, we are broke. Are you tired of wrestling over and over again with the same old concerns? Has it become aggravating to the point it is beginning to weigh you down? 1 Peter 5:7 says, "Cast all your anxiety on him because he cares for us." Just throw it on him and let him carry your burdens. Jesus said we could cast all of our cares on him because he cares for us! There is nothing we are going through that we cannot cast on the Lord. By prayer, meditation, and practicing the principles given in this chapter, you can learn how to truly have...

No Worries.

(All citations ESV unless otherwise noted)

Be strong and courageous. Do not fear or be in dread of them, for it is the Lord your God who goes with you. He will not leave you or forsake you" (Deuteronomy 31:6).

It is the Lord who goes before you. He will be with you; he will not leave you or forsake you. Do not fear or be dismayed (Deuteronomy 31:8).

Have I not commanded you? Be strong and courageous. Do not be frightened, and do not be dismayed, for the Lord your God is with you wherever you go (Joshua 1:9).

Then Job arose and tore his robe and shaved his head and fell on the ground and worshiped. And he said, "Naked I came from my mother's womb, and naked shall I return. The Lord gave, and the Lord has taken away; blessed be the name of the Lord" (Job 1:20-21).

I have set the Lord always before me; because he is at my right hand, I shall not be shaken (Psalms 16:8).

A Psalm of David. The Lord is my shepherd; I shall not want. He makes me lie down in green pastures. He leads me beside still waters. He restores my soul. He leads me in paths of righteousness for his name's sake. Even though I walk through the valley of the shadow of death, I will fear no evil, for you are with me; your rod and your staff, they comfort me. You prepare a table before me in the presence of my enemies; you anoint my head with oil; my cup overflows (Psalms 23:1-6).

Of David. The Lord is my light and my salvation; whom shall I fear? The Lord is the stronghold of my life; of whom shall I be afraid? (Psalms 27:1).

I sought the Lord, and he answered me and delivered me from all my fears (Psalms 34:4).

When the righteous cry for help, the Lord hears and delivers them out of all their troubles. The Lord is near to the brokenhearted and saves the crushed in spirit. Many are the afflictions of the righteous, but the Lord delivers him out of them all (Psalms 34:17-19).

Be still before the Lord and wait patiently for him; fret not yourself over the one who prospers in his way, over the man who carries out evil devices! Refrain from anger and forsake wrath! Fret not yourself; it tends only to evil. For the evildoers shall be cut off, but those who wait for the Lord shall inherit the land (Psalms 37:7-9).

Of David. Fret not yourself because of evildoers; be not envious of wrongdoers! (Psalms 37:1).

I have been young, and now am old, yet I have not seen the righteous forsaken or his children begging for bread (Psalms 37:25).

O Lord, all my longing is before you; my sighing is not hidden from you (Psalms 38:9).

To the choirmaster. Of the Sons of Korah. According to Alamoth. A Song. God is our refuge and strength, a very present help in trouble (Psalms 46:1).

"Be still and know that I am God. I will be exalted among the nations; I will be exalted in the earth!" (Psalms 46:10).

Cast your burden on the Lord, and he will sustain you; he will never permit the righteous to be moved (Psalms 55:22).

When I am afraid, I put my trust in you. In God, whose word I praise, in God I trust; I shall not be afraid. What can flesh do to me? (Psalms 56:3-4).

He who dwells in the shelter of the Most High will abide in the shadow of the Almighty. I will say to the Lord, "My refuge and my fortress, my God, in whom I trust." For he will deliver you from the snare of the fowler and from the deadly pestilence (Psalms 91:1-3).

When the cares of my heart are many, your consolations cheer my soul (Psalms 94:19).

A Song of Ascents. I lift up my eyes to the hills. From where does my help come? My help comes from the Lord, who made heaven and earth (Psalms 121:1-2).

The Lord will fulfill his purpose for me; your steadfast love, O Lord, endures forever. Do not forsake the work of your hands (Psalms 138:8).

Trust in the Lord with all your heart, and do not lean on your own understanding. In all your ways acknowledge him, and he will make straight your paths (Proverbs 3:5-6).

Anxiety in a man's heart weighs him down, but a good word makes him glad (Proverbs 12:25).

The fear of man lays a snare, but whoever trusts in the Lord is safe (Proverbs 29:25).

You keep him in perfect peace whose mind is stayed on you, because he trusts in you (Isaiah 26:3-4).

Say to those who have an anxious heart, "Be strong, fear not! Behold, your God will come with vengeance, with the recompense of God. He will come and save you" (Isaiah 35:3-4).

Fear not, for I am with you; be not dismayed, for I am your God; I will strengthen you, I will help you, I will uphold you with my righteous right hand (Isaiah 41:10).

For I, the Lord your God, hold your right hand; it is I who say to you, "Fear not, I am the one who helps you" (Isaiah 41:13).

But they who wait for the Lord shall renew their strength; they shall mount up with wings like eagles; they shall run and not be weary; they shall walk and not faint (Isaiah 40:31).

Blessed is the man who trusts in the Lord, whose trust is the Lord. He is like a tree planted by water, that sends out its roots by the stream, and does not fear when heat comes, for its leaves remain green, and is not anxious in the year of drought, for it does not cease to bear fruit (Jeremiah 17:7-8).

For I know the plans I have for you, declares the Lord, plans for welfare and not for evil, to give you a future and a hope (Jeremiah 29:11).

When God saw what they did, how they turned from their evil way, God relented of the disaster that he had said he would do to them, and he did not do it (Jonah 3:10).

Beware of practicing your righteousness before other people in order to be seen by them, for then you will have no reward from your Father who is in heaven. "Thus, when you give to the needy, sound no trumpet before you, as the hypocrites do in the synagogues and in the streets, that they may be praised by others. Truly, I say to you, they have received their reward. But when you give to the needy, do not let your left hand know what your right hand is doing, so that your giving may be in secret. And your Father who sees in secret will reward you. "And when you pray, you must not be like the hypocrites. For they love to stand and pray in the synagogues and at the street corners, that they may be seen by others. Truly, I say to you, they have received their reward (Matthew 6:1-4).

"Therefore, I tell you, do not be anxious about your life, what you will eat or what you will drink, nor about your body, what you will put on. Is not life more than food, and the body more than clothing? Look at the birds of the air: they neither sow nor reap nor gather into barns, and yet your heavenly Father feeds them. Are you not of more value than they? And which of you by being anxious can add a single hour to his span of life? And why are you anxious about clothing? Consider the lilies of the field, how they grow: they neither toil nor spin, yet I tell you, even Solomon in all his glory was not arrayed like one of these. For the Gentiles seek after all these things, and your heavenly Father knows that you need them all. But seek first the kingdom of God and his righteousness, and all these things will be added to you. Therefore, do not be anxious about tomorrow, for tomorrow will be anxious for itself. Sufficient for the day is its own trouble (Matthew 6:25-34).

Come to me, all who labor and are heavy laden, and I will give you rest. Take my yoke upon you, and learn from me, for I am gentle and lowly in heart, and you will find rest for your souls. For my yoke is easy, and my burden is light (Matthew 11:28-30).

As for what was sown among thorns, this is the one who hears the word, but the cares of the world and the deceitfulness of riches choke the word, and it proves unfruitful (Matthew 13:22).

Jesus immediately reached out his hand and took hold of him, saying to him, "O you of little faith, why did you doubt?" (Matthew 14:31).

But Jesus, aware of this, said, "O you of little faith, why are you discussing among yourselves the fact that you have no bread? (Matthew 16:8).

And when they bring you to trial and deliver you over, do not be anxious beforehand what you are to say, but say whatever is given you in that hour, for it is not you who speak, but the Holy Spirit (Mark 13:11).

For nothing will be impossible with God (Luke 1:37).

But the Lord answered her, "Martha, Martha, you are anxious and troubled about many things, but one thing is necessary. Mary has chosen the good portion, which will not be taken away from her (Luke 10:41-42).

And he said to his disciples, "Therefore I tell you, do not be anxious about your life, what you will eat, nor about your body, what you will put on. For life is more than food, and the body more than clothing. Consider the ravens: they neither sow nor reap, they have neither storehouse nor barn, and yet God feeds them. Of how much more value are you than the birds! And which of you by being anxious can add a single hour to his span of life? If then you are not able to do as small a thing as that, why are you anxious about the rest? (Luke 12:22-34).

Settle it therefore in your minds not to meditate beforehand how to answer (Luke 21:14).

But watch yourselves lest your hearts be weighed down with dissipation and drunkenness and cares of this life, and that day come upon you suddenly like a trap (Luke 21:34).

For God so loved the world, that he gave his only Son, that whoever believes in him should not perish but have eternal life. For God did not send his Son into the world to condemn the world, but in order that the world might be saved through him (NIV, John 3:16-17).

Peace, I leave with you; my peace I give to you. Not as the world gives do I give to you. Let not your hearts be troubled, neither let them be afraid (John 14:27).

I have said these things to you, that in me you may have peace. In the world, you will have tribulation. But take heart; I have overcome the world (John 16:33).

For to set the mind on the flesh is death, but to set the mind on the Spirit is life and peace (Romans 8:6).

And we know that for those who love God all things work together for good, for those who are called according to his purpose (Romans 8:28).

What then shall we say to these things? If God is for us, who can be against us? He who did not spare his own Son but gave him up for us all, how will he not also with him graciously give us all things? (Romans 8:31-32).

For I am sure that neither death nor life, nor angels nor rulers, nor things present nor things to come, nor powers, nor height nor depth, nor anything else in all creation, will be able to separate us from the love of God in Christ Jesus our Lord (Romans 8:38-39).

May the God of hope fill you with all joy and peace in believing, so that by the power of the Holy Spirit you may abound in hope (Romans 15:13).

Or do you not know that your body is a temple of the Holy Spirit within you, whom you have from God? You are not your own, for you were bought with a price. So, glorify God in your body (1 Corinthians 6:19-20).

No temptation has overtaken you that is not common to man. God is faithful, and he will not let you be tempted beyond your ability, but with the temptation he will also provide the way of escape, that you may be able to endure it (1 Corinthians 10:13).

And God is able to make all grace abound to you, so that having all sufficiency in all things at all times, you may abound in every good work (2 Corinthians 9:8).

For the sake of Christ, then, I am content with weaknesses, insults, hardships, persecutions, and calamities. For when I am weak, then I am strong (2 Corinthians 12:10).

And let us not grow weary of doing good, for in due season we will reap, if we do not give up (Galatians 6:9).

Let no corrupting talk come out of your mouths, but only such as is good for building up, as fits the occasion, that it may give grace to those who hear (Ephesians 4:29).

Do not be anxious about anything, but in everything by prayer and supplication with thanksgiving let your requests be made known to God. And the peace of God, which surpasses all understanding, will guard your hearts and your minds in Christ Jesus (Philippians 4:6-7).

I can do all things through him who strengthens me (Philippians 4:13).

And my God will supply every need of yours according to his riches in glory in Christ Jesus (Philippians 4:19).

Set your mind on things that are above, not on things that are on earth (Colossians 3:2).

And let the peace of Christ rule in your hearts, to which indeed you were called in one body. And be thankful (Colossians 3:15).

Now may the Lord of peace himself give you peace at all times in every way. The Lord be with you all (NIV, 2 Thessalonians 3:16).

For God gave us a spirit not of fear but of power and love and self-control (2 Timothy 1:7).

Now faith is the assurance of things hoped for, the conviction of things not seen (Hebrews 11:1).

Keep your life free from the love of money, and be content with what you have, for he has said, "I will never leave you nor forsake you." So, we can confidently say, "The Lord is my helper; I will not fear; what can man do to me?" (Hebrews 13:5-6).

James, a servant of God and of the Lord Jesus Christ, To the twelve tribes in the Dispersion: Greetings. Count it all joy, my brothers, when you meet trials of various kinds, for you know that the testing of your faith produces steadfastness. And let steadfastness have its full effect, that you may be perfect and complete, lacking in nothing. If any of you lacks wisdom, let him ask God, who gives generously to all without reproach, and it will be given him (James 1:1-27).

But even if you should suffer for righteousness' sake, you will be blessed. Have no fear of them, nor be troubled (1 Peter 3:14).

Humble yourselves, therefore, under the mighty hand of God so that at the proper time he may exalt you, casting all your anxieties on him, because he cares for you (1 Peter 5:6-7).

There is no fear in love, but perfect love casts out fear. For fear has to do with punishment, and whoever fears has not been perfected in love (1 John 4:18).

The revelation of Jesus Christ, which God gave him to show to his servants the things that must soon take place. He made it known by sending his angel to his servant John (Revelation 1:1).

And I heard a loud voice from the throne saying, "Behold, the dwelling place of God is with man. He will dwell with them, and they will be his people, and God himself will be with them as their God. He will wipe away every tear from their eyes, and death shall be no more, neither shall there be mourning, nor crying, nor pain anymore, for the former things have passed away." (Revelation 21:3-4).

CHAPTER SEVEN
The Child Welfare Act

The Little Children and Jesus

One day children were brought to Jesus in the hope that he would lay hands on them and pray over them. The disciples shooed them off. But Jesus intervened: "Let the children alone, don't prevent them from coming to me. God's kingdom is made up of people like these" (MSG, Matthew 19:13-15).

In childhood and youth, the character is most impressible. The power of self–control should then be acquired. By the fireside and at the family board influences are exerted whose results are as enduring as eternity. More than any natural endowment, the habits established in early years decide whether a man will be victorious or vanquished in the battle of life. Youth is the sowing time. It determines the character of the harvest, for this life and the life to come.

— Ellen G. White

A Parent's Prayer for Their Children
Loving God,
You are the giver of all we possess,
the source of all of our blessings.
We thank and praise you.
Thank you for the gift of our children.
Help us to set boundaries for them,
and yet encourage them to explore.
Give us the strength and courage to treat
each day as a fresh start.
May our children come to know you, the one true God,
and Jesus Christ, whom you have sent.
May your Holy Spirit help them to grow
in faith, hope, and love,
so, they may know peace, truth, and goodness.
May their ears hear your voice.
May their eyes see your presence in all things.
May their lips proclaim your word.
May their hearts be your dwelling place.
May their hands do works of charity.
May their feet walk in the way of Jesus Christ,
your Son and our Lord.
Amen.

— Source Unknown

A Parent's Prayer
Heavenly Father,
Make me a better parent.
Teach me to understand my children,
To listen patiently to what they have to say,
And to answer all their questions kindly.
Keep me from interrupting them,
or contradicting them.
Make me as courteous to them,
as I would have them be to me.
Forbid that I should ever laugh at their mistakes,
Or resort to shame or ridicule if they displease me.
Bless me with the bigness to grant them
all their reasonable requests,
And the courage to deny them privileges
that I know will do them harm.
Make me fair and just and kind.
And fit me, O Lord,
to be loved and respected
and imitated by my children.
Amen.

— Source Unknown

(All citations NIV)

These commandments that I give you today are to be on your hearts. Impress them on your children. Talk about them when you sit at home and when you walk along the road, when you lie down and when you get up (Deuteronomy 6:7).

For he will command his angels concerning you to guard you in all your ways (Psalms 91:11).

Discipline your children, for in that there is hope. Do not be a willing party to their death (Proverbs 19:18).

Start children off on the way they should go, and even when they are old, they will not turn from it (Proverbs 22:6).

A rod and a reprimand impart wisdom, but a child left undisciplined disgraces its mother (Proverbs 29:15).

Discipline your children, and they will give you peace; they will bring you the delights you desire (Proverbs 29:17).

See that you do not despise one of these little ones. For I tell you that their angels in heaven always see the face of my Father in heaven (Matthew 18:10).

Then people brought little children to Jesus for him to place his hands on them and pray for them. But the disciples rebuked them. Jesus said, "Let the little children come to me, and do not hinder them, for the kingdom of heaven belongs to such as these." When he had placed his hands on them, he went on from there (Matthew 19:13-15).

Fathers do not embitter your children, or they will become

discouraged (Colossians 3:21).

CHAPTER EIGHT

In God We Trust (Getcha Money Right)

"It's not what you gather, but what you scatter..."

— Helen Walton

"I bargain with Life for a penny,
    And Life would pay no more,
    However, I begged at evening
    When I counted my scanty store.
    For Life is a just employer,
    He gives you what you ask,
    But once you set the wages,
    Why, you must bear the task.
    I worked for a menial's hire,
    Only to learn, dismayed,
    That any wage I had asked of Life,
    Life would have willing paid"

— Napoleon Hill - Think and Grow Rich

OK, Now let's talk about something that always gets everyone's attention.

MONEY! Also known as bread, moolah, dinero, loot, and cold hard cash. Yes, God speaks a great deal on the subject of money in the Bible. He talks about How to get it, how to use it, how to keep it, and how to lose it. Getting your money right is not only about making money but, it's more about the right attitude in your relationship with God and others. The Bible says, in Matthew 6:33, "But seek (aim at and strive after) first of all His kingdom and His righteousness (His way of doing and being right), and then all these things taken together will be given you besides." Also, as a bonus feature in this chapter, we will look at debt and what God has to say about that as well. As people of the God who has cattle on a thousand hills, the maker of heaven and earth, the one who has all power in His hand there is no reason we should be lacking for anything, especially money. And we certainly shouldn't be slaves to debt when Jesus paid our ransom with His very own precious blood to set us free from sin and death. The Bible says, "the thief (Devil) comes only in order to steal and kill and destroy. I came that they may have and enjoy life, and have it in abundance [to the full, till it overflows]" (AMP, John 10:10).

Now turn the page, read God's Word on the matter, put the Word into action, and...

Getcha Money Right!

(All citations NIV unless otherwise noted)

If you lend money to any of my people with you who is poor, you shall not be like a moneylender to him, and you shall not exact interest from him (Exodus 22:25).

You shall remember the Lord your God, for it is he who gives you power to get wealth, that he may confirm his covenant that he swore to your fathers, as it is this day (Deuteronomy 8:18).

Every man shall give as he is able, according to the blessing of the Lord your God that he has given you (Deuteronomy 16:17).

But who am I, and what is my people, that we should be able thus to offer willingly? For all things come from you, and of your own have we given you (1 Chronicles 29:14).

A Psalm of David. The earth is the Lord's and the fullness thereof, the world and those who dwell therein (Psalms 24:1).

The wicked borrows but does not pay back, but the righteous is generous and gives (Psalms 37:21).

Honor the Lord with your wealth and with the first fruits of all your produce (Proverbs 3:9).

A slack hand causes poverty, but the hand of the diligent makes rich (Proverbs 10:4).

The blessing of the Lord makes rich, and he adds no sorrow with it (Proverbs 10:22).

A false balance is an abomination to the Lord, but a just weight is his delight (Proverbs 11:1).

Riches do not profit in the day of wrath, but righteousness delivers from death (Proverbs 11:4).

Whoever trusts in his riches will fall, but the righteous will flourish like a green leaf (Proverbs 11:28).

Wealth gained hastily will dwindle, but whoever gathers little by little will increase it (Proverbs 13:11).

A good man leaves an inheritance to his children's children, but the sinner's wealth is laid up for the righteous (Proverbs 13:22).

Whoever is greedy for unjust gain troubles his own household, but he who hates bribes will live (Proverbs 15:27).

The rich think their money is a wall of protection (CEV, Proverbs 18:11).

Precious treasure and oil are in a wise man's dwelling, but a foolish man devours it (Proverbs 21:20).

A good name is to be chosen rather than great riches, and favor is better than silver or gold (Proverbs 22:1).

The plans of the diligent lead surely to abundance, but everyone who is hasty comes only to poverty (Proverbs 21:5).

The rich rules over the poor, and the borrower is the slave of the lender (Proverbs 22:7).

Give up trying so hard to get rich (CEV, Proverbs 23:4).

Your money flies away before you know it, just like an eagle suddenly taking off (CEV, Proverbs 23:5).

Riches can disappear fast. And the king's crown doesn't stay in his family forever—so watch your business interests closely. Know the state of your flocks and your herds (TLB, Proverbs 27:23-24).

Whoever multiplies his wealth by interest and profit gathers it for him who is generous to the poor (Proverbs 28:8).

A faithful man will abound with blessings, but whoever hastens to be rich will not go unpunished (Proverbs 28:20).

A stingy man hastens after wealth and does not know that poverty will come upon him (Proverbs 28:22).

He who loves money will not be satisfied with money, nor he who loves wealth with his income; this also is vanity (Ecclesiastes 5:10).

For the protection of wisdom is like the protection of money, and the advantage of knowledge is that wisdom preserves the life of him who has it (Ecclesiastes 7:12).

"Will a man rob God? Surely not! And yet you have robbed me. 'What do you mean? When did we ever rob you?' You have robbed me of the tithes and offerings due me. And so the awesome curse of God is cursing you, for your whole nation has been robbing me. Bring all the tithes into the storehouse so that there will be food enough in my Temple; if you do, I will open up the windows of heaven for you and pour out a blessing so great you won't have room enough to take it in! Try it! Let me prove it to you! Your crops will be large, for I will guard them from insects and plagues. Your grapes won't shrivel away before they ripen," says the Lord Almighty. "And all nations will call you blessed, for you will be a land sparkling with happiness. These are the promises of the Lord Almighty (TLB, Malachi 3: 8-12).

"Give to the one who begs from you and do not refuse the one who would borrow from you" (Matthew 5:42).

"For where your treasure is, there your heart will be also" (Matthew 6:21).

No one can serve two masters, for either he will hate the one and love the other, or he will be devoted to the one and despise the other. You cannot serve God and money. Therefore, I tell you, do not be anxious about your life, what you will eat or what you will drink, nor about your body, what you will put on. Is not life more than food, and the body more than clothing? (Matthew 6:25).

But seek first the kingdom of God and his righteousness, and all these things will be added to you (Matthew 6:33).

Jesus said to him, "If you would be perfect, go, sell what you possess and give to the poor, and you will have treasure in heaven; and come, follow me" (Matthew 19:21).

His master said to him, "Well done, good and faithful servant. You have been faithful over a little; I will set you over much. Enter into the joy of your master" (Matthew 25:21).

But the cares of the world and the deceitfulness of riches and the desires for other things enter in and choke the word, and it proves unfruitful (Mark 4:19).

For what does it profit a man to gain the whole world and forfeit his soul? (Mark 8:36).

Give, and it will be given to you. They will pour into your lap a good measure—pressed down, shaken together, and running over [with no space left for more]. For with the standard of measurement you use [when you do good to others], it will be measured to you in return (AMP, Luke 6:38).

And he said to them, "Take care, and be on your guard against all covetousness, for one's life does not consist in the abundance of his possessions" (Luke 12:15).

For where your treasure is, there will your heart be also (Luke 12:34).

For which of you, desiring to build a tower, does not first sit down and count the cost, whether he has enough to complete it? (Luke 14:28).

If then you have not been faithful in the unrighteous wealth, who will entrust to you the true riches? (Luke 16:11).

For God so loved the world, that he gave his only Son, that whoever believes in him should not perish but have eternal life (John 3:16).

In all things I have shown you that by working hard in this way we must help the weak and remember the words of the Lord Jesus, how he himself said, "It is more blessed to give than to receive" (Acts 20:35).

On the first day of every week, each of you is to put something aside and store it up, as he may prosper, so that there will be no collecting when I come (1 Corinthians 16:2).

And God is able to make all grace abound to you, so that having all sufficiency in all things at all times, you may abound in every good work (2 Corinthians 9:8).

For you may be sure of this, that everyone who is sexually immoral or impure, or who is covetous (that is, an idolater), has no inheritance in the kingdom of Christ and God (Ephesians 5:5).

Do not be anxious about anything, but in everything by prayer and supplication with thanksgiving, let your requests be made known to God (Philippians 4:6).

I can do all things through him who strengthens me (Philippians 4:13).

And my God will supply every need of yours according to his riches in glory in Christ Jesus (Philippians 4:19).

Every good gift and every perfect gift is from above, coming down from the Father of lights with whom there is no variation or shadow due to change (James 1:17).

Keep your life free from love of money, and be content with what you have, for he has said, "I will never leave you nor forsake you" (Hebrews 13:5).

Casting all your anxieties on him, because he cares for you (1 Peter 5:7).

But if anyone does not provide for his relatives, and especially for members of his household, he has denied the faith and is worse than an unbeliever (1 Timothy 5:8).

For the love of money is a root of all kinds of evils. It is through this craving that some have wandered away from the faith and pierced themselves with many pangs (1 Timothy 6:10).

As for the rich in this present age, charge them not to be haughty, nor to set their hopes on the uncertainty of riches, but on God, who richly provides us with everything to enjoy (1 Timothy 6:17).

Beloved, I pray that all may go well with you and that you may be in good health, as it goes well with your soul (3 John 1:2).

Be Debt Free

For the Lord your God will bless you as he has promised, and you will lend to many nations but will borrow from none. You will rule over many nations, but none will rule over you (Deuteronomy 15:6).

The wicked borrow and do not repay, but the righteous give generously (Psalms 37:21).

Do not withhold good from those to whom it is due when it is in your power to act (Proverbs 3:27).

Dishonest money dwindles away, but whoever gathers money little by little makes it grow (Proverbs 13:11).

The rich rule over the poor, and the borrower is slave to the lender (Proverbs 22:7).

And forgive us our debts, as we also have forgiven our debtors (Matthew 6:12).

No one can serve two masters. Either you will hate the one and love the other, or you will be devoted to the one and despise the other. You cannot serve both God and money (Matthew 6:24).

Give to everyone who asks you, and if anyone takes what belongs to you, do not demand it back (Luke 6:30).

Suppose one of you wants to build a tower. Won't you first sit down and estimate the cost to see if you have enough money to complete it? (Luke 14:28).

Pay to all what is owed to them: taxes to whom taxes are owed, revenue to whom revenue is owed, respect to whom respect is owed, honor to whom honor is owed. Owe no one anything, except to love each other, for the one who loves another has fulfilled the law (Romans 13:7-8).

Keep your lives free from the love of money and be content with what you have, because God has said, "Never will I leave you; never will I forsake you" (Hebrews 13:5).

CHAPTER NINE

Free Health Plan

Great medical care is priceless. Did you know there's a way to avoid a lot of illnesses that have unnecessarily snuffed out the lives of so many people?

Take care of your body. Those in the medical field have warned us about cholesterol, tobacco, stress, obesity, and alcohol. God truly cares about us and how we treat our bodies, and He gives us a free health plan to go by: the Bible. In this chapter, there are biblical scriptures about how we can have abundant health and a longer life.

And God said, Behold, I have given you every herb bearing seed, which is upon the face of all the earth, and every tree, in the which is the fruit of a tree yielding seed; to you it shall be for meat (KJV, Genesis 1:29).

The Lord is my strength, the reason for my song, because he has saved me. I praise and honor the Lord—he is my God and the God of my ancestors (CEV, Exodus 15:2).

Then he said, "I am the Lord your God, and I cure your diseases. If you obey me by doing right and by following my laws and teachings, I won't punish you with the diseases I sent on the Egyptians" (CEV, Exodus 15:26).

Remember that the Sabbath Day belongs to me. You have six days when you can do your work, but the seventh day of each week belongs to me, your God. No one is to work on that day—not you, your children, your slaves, your animals, or the foreigners who live in your towns. In six days I made the sky, the earth, the oceans, and everything in them, but on the seventh day I rested. That's why I made the Sabbath a special day that belongs to me (CEV, Exodus 20:8-11).

Worship only me, the Lord your God! I will bless you with plenty of food and water and keep you strong (CEV, Exodus 23:25).

Work for six days and rest on the seventh day, even during the seasons for plowing and harvesting (CEV, Exodus 34:21).

Clean and Unclean Animals

The Lord told Moses and Aaron to say to the community of Israel: You may eat any animal that has divided hoofs and chews the cud. But you must not eat animals such as camels, rock badgers, and rabbits that chew the cud but don't have divided hoofs. And you must not eat pigs—they have divided hoofs, but don't chew the cud. All of these animals are unclean, and you are forbidden even to touch their dead bodies. You may eat anything that lives in water and has fins and scales. But it would be disgusting for you to eat anything else that lives in water, and you must not even touch their dead bodies. Eagles, vultures, buzzards, crows, ostriches, hawks, sea gulls, owls, pelicans, storks, herons, hoopoes, and bats are also disgusting, and you are forbidden to eat any of them. The only winged insects you may eat are locusts, grasshoppers, and crickets. All other winged insects that crawl are too disgusting for you to eat. Don't even touch the dead bodies of animals that have divided hoofs but don't chew the cud. And don't touch the dead bodies of animals that have paws. If you do, you must wash your clothes, but you are still unclean until evening. Moles, rats, mice, and all kinds of lizards are unclean. Anyone who touches their dead bodies, or anything touched by their dead bodies becomes unclean until evening. If something made of wood, cloth, or leather touches one of their dead bodies, it must be washed, but it is still unclean until evening. If any of these animals is found dead in a clay pot, the pot must be broken to pieces, and everything in it becomes unclean. If you pour water from this pot on any food, that food becomes unclean, and anything drinkable in the pot becomes unclean. If the dead body of one of these animals' touches anything else, including ovens and stoves, that thing becomes unclean and must be destroyed. A spring or a cistern where one of these dead animals is found is still clean, but anyone who touches the animal becomes unclean. If the dead body of one of these animals is found lying on seeds that have been set aside for planting, the seeds remain clean. But seeds that are soaking in water become unclean, if the dead animal is found in the water. If an animal that may be eaten happens to die, and you touch it, you become unclean until evening. If you eat any of its meat or carry its body away, you must wash your clothes, but you are still unclean until evening. Don't eat any of those disgusting little creatures that crawl or walk close to the ground.

If you eat any of them, you will become just as disgusting and unclean as they are. I am the Lord your God, and you must dedicate yourselves to me and be holy, just as I am holy. Don't become disgusting by eating any of these unclean creatures. I brought you out of Egypt so that I could be your God. Now you must become holy because I am holy! (CEV, Leviticus 11:1-45).

I pray that the Lord will bless and protect you and that he will show you mercy and kindness. May the Lord be good to you and give you peace (CEV, Numbers 6:24-26).

You will no longer suffer with the same horrible diseases that you sometimes had in Egypt. You will be healthy, but the Lord will make your enemies suffer from those diseases (CEV, Deuteronomy 7:15).

Moses said to Israel:

Today I am giving you the laws and teachings of the Lord your God. Always obey them, and the Lord will make Israel the most famous and important nation on earth, and he will bless you in many ways. The Lord will make your businesses and your farms successful. You will have many children. You will harvest large crops, and your herds of cattle and flocks of sheep and goats will produce many young. You will have plenty of bread to eat. The Lord will make you successful in your daily work. The Lord will help you defeat your enemies and make them scatter in all directions. The Lord your God is giving you the land, and he will make sure you are successful in everything you do. Your harvests will be so large that your storehouses will be full. If you follow and obey the Lord, he will make you his own special people, just as he promised. Then everyone on earth will know that you belong to the Lord, and they will be afraid of you. The Lord will give you a lot of children and make sure that your animals give birth to many young. The Lord promised your ancestors that this land would be yours, and he will make it produce large crops for you. The Lord will open the storehouses of the skies where he keeps the rain, and he will send rain on your land at just the right times. He will make you successful in everything you do. You will have plenty of money to lend to other nations, but you won't need to borrow any yourself. Obey the laws and teachings that I'm giving you today, and the Lord your God will make Israel a leader among the nations, and not a follower. Israel will be wealthy and powerful, not poor and weak. But you must not reject any of his laws and teachings or worship other gods (CEV, Deuteronomy 28.1-14; Leviticus 26.3-13).

Don't you understand? I am the only God; there are no others. I am the one who takes life and gives it again. I punished you with suffering. But now I will heal you and nothing can stop me! (CEV, Deuteronomy 32:39).

If my own people will humbly pray and turn back to me and stop sinning, then I will answer them from heaven. I will forgive them and make their land fertile once again. I will hear the prayers made in this temple (CEV, 2 Chronicles 7:14-15).

You, Lord, are the one I praise. So, heal me and rescue me! Then I will be completely well and perfectly safe (CEV, Jeremiah 17:14).

His flesh shall be fresher than a child's; he shall return to the days of his youth (KJV, Job 33:25).

And the inhabitant shall not say, I am sick: the people that dwell therein shall be forgiven their iniquity (KJV, Isaiah 33:24).

But they that wait upon the Lord shall renew their strength; they shall mount up with wings as eagles; they shall run, and not be weary, and they shall walk, and not faint (KJV, Isaiah 40:31).

Have pity on me and heal my feeble body. My bones tremble with fear (CEV, Psalms 6:2).

I trust your love, and I feel like celebrating because you rescued me. You have been good to me; Lord and I will sing about you (CEV, Psalm 13:5-6).

He is my strength, my shield from every danger. I trusted in him, and he helped me. Joy rises in my heart until I burst out in songs of praise to him (TLB, Psalm 28:7).

The Lord will give strength unto his people; the Lord will bless his people with peace (KJV, Psalms 29:11).

O Lord my God, I cried unto thee, and thou hast healed me (KJV, Psalms 30:2).

Hear me, Lord; oh, have pity and help me. Then he turned my sorrow into joy! He took away my clothes of mourning and clothed me with joy (TLB, Psalms 30:10-11).

Night and day, your hand weighed heavily on me, and my strength was gone as in the summer heat. So I confessed my sins and told them all to you. I said, "I'll tell the Lord each one of my sins. " Then you forgave me and took away my guilt (CEV, Psalms 32:4-5).

When his people pray for help, he listens and rescues them from their troubles. The Lord is there to rescue all who are discouraged and have given up hope. The Lord's people may suffer a lot, but he will always bring them safely through. Not one of their bones will ever be broken. Wicked people are killed by their own evil deeds, and if you hate God's people, you will be punished. The Lord saves the lives of his servants. Run to him for protection, and you won't be punished (CEV, Psalms 34:17-22).

My body hurts all over because of your anger. Even my bones are in pain and my sins (CEV, Psalms 38:3).

You protect them and keep them alive. You make them happy here in this land, and you don't hand them over to their enemies. You always heal them and restore their strength when they are sick (CEV, Psalms 41:2-3).

The Lord will sustain, refresh, and strengthen him on his bed of languishing; all his bed You [O Lord] will turn, change, and transform in his illness (AMPC, Psalms 41:3).

I said, Lord, be merciful unto me: heal my soul; for I have sinned against thee (KJV, Psalms 41:4).

You are my God. I am deeply discouraged, and so I think about you here where the Jordan begins at Mount Hermon and at Mount Mizar (CEV, Psalms 42:6).

But, O my soul, don't be discouraged. Don't be upset. Expect God to act! For I know that I shall again have plenty of reason to praise him for all that he will do. He is my help! He is my God! (TLB, Psalms 42:11).

That thy way may be known upon earth, thy saving health among all nations (KJV, Psalms 67:2).

My health fails; my spirits droop, yet God remains! He is the strength of my heart; he is mine forever! (TLB, Psalms 73:26).

Bless the Lord, O my soul, and forget not all his benefits: Who forgiveth all thine iniquities; who healeth all thy diseases; Who redeemeth thy life from destruction; who crowneth thee with loving kindness and tender mercies (KJV, Psalms 103:2-4).

The Lord forgives our sins, heals us when we are sick, and protects us from death. His kindness and love are a crown on our heads. Each day that we live, he provides for our needs and gives us the strength of a young eagle. For all who are mistreated, the Lord brings justice (CEV, Psalms 103:3-6).

Then they cried out to the Lord in their trouble, And He saved them from their distresses. He sent His word and healed them and rescued them from their destruction. Let them give thanks to the Lord for His loving kindness, and for His wonderful acts to the children of men! (AMP, Psalms 107:19-21).

By the power of his own word, he healed you and saved you from destruction (CEV, Psalms 107:20).

The Lord Will Bless You if You Obey

The Lord is my strength and song and is become my salvation (KJV, Psalms 118:14).

I won't ever forget your teachings because you give me new life when I follow them (CEV, Psalms 119:93).

Look deep into my heart, God, and find out everything I am thinking. Don't let me follow evil ways, but lead me in the way that time has proven true (CEV, Psalms 139:23-24).

He heals the brokenhearted and binds up their wounds, healing their pain and comforting their sorrow (AMP, Psalms 147:3).

The Lord is pleased with his people, and he gives victory to those who are humble (CEV, Psalms 149:4).

My son, forget not my law or teaching, but let your heart keep my commandments. For length of days and years of a life [worth living] and tranquility [inward and outward and continuing through old age till death], these shall they add to you (AMPC, Proverbs 3:1-2).

With all your heart, you must trust the Lord and not your own judgment. Always let him lead you, and he will clear the road for you to follow. Don't ever think that you are wise enough, but respect the Lord and stay away from evil. This will make you healthy, and you will feel strong (CEV, Proverbs 3:5-8).

My son, attend to my words; incline thine ear unto my sayings. Let them not depart from thine eyes; keep them in the midst of thine heart. For they are life unto those that find them, and health to all their flesh (KJV, Proverbs 4:20-22).

Sharp words cut like a sword, but words of wisdom heal (CEV, Proverbs 12:18).

Hope deferred maketh the heart sick: but when the desire cometh, it is a tree of life (KJV, Proverbs 13:12).

A wicked messenger falleth into mischief: but a faithful ambassador is health (KJV, Proverbs 13:17).

A calm and undisturbed mind and heart are the life and health of the body, but envy, jealousy, and wrath are like rottenness of the bone (AMP, Proverbs 14:30).

Kind words are like honey. They cheer you up and make you feel strong (CEV, Proverbs 16:24).

A happy heart is good medicine, and a cheerful mind works healing, but a broken spirit dries up the bones (AMP, Proverbs 17:22).

Words of Wisdom Are Better than Gold.

There is none to plead thy cause, that thou mayest be bound up: thou hast no healing medicines (CEV, Proverbs 20:1).

Don't be a heavy drinker or stuff yourself with food. It will make you feel drowsy, and you will end up poor with only rags to wear (CEV, Proverbs 23:20-21).

Have you found [pleasure sweet like] honey? Eat only as much as is sufficient for you, lest, being filled with it, you vomit it (AMPC, Proverbs 25:16).

She girds herself with strength [spiritual, mental, and physical fitness for her God-given task] and makes her arms strong and firm (AMP, Proverbs 31:17).

To everything there is a season, and a time for every matter or purpose under heaven: A time to be born and a time to die, a time to plant and a time to pluck up what is planted. A time to kill and a time to heal, a time to break down and a time to build up. A time to weep and a time to laugh, a time to mourn and a time to dance. A time to cast away stones and a time to gather stones together, a time to embrace and a time to refrain from embracing. A time to get and a time to lose, a time to keep and a time to cast away. A time to rend and a time to sew, a time to keep silence and a time to speak. A time to love and a time to hate, a time for war and a time for peace (AMPC, Ecclesiastes 3:1-8).

Therefore, remove [the lusts that end in] sorrow and vexation from your heart and mind and put away evil from your body, for youth and the dawn of life are vanity [transitory, idle, empty], and devoid of truth (AMPC, Ecclesiastes 11:10).

All has been heard; the end of the matter is: Fear God [revere and worship Him, knowing that He is] and keep His commandments, for this is the whole of man [the full, original purpose of his creation, the object of God's providence, the root of character, the foundation of all happiness, the adjustment to all inharmonious circumstances and conditions under the sun] and the whole [duty] for every man (AMPC, Ecclesiastes 12:13).

At that time you will say, "I thank you, Lord! You were angry with me, but you stopped being angry and gave me comfort. I trust you to save me, Lord God, and I won't be afraid. My power and my strength come from you, and you have saved me." With great joy, you people will get water from the well of victory (CEV, Isaiah 12:1-3).

After the Lord has punished Egypt, the people will turn to him. Then he will answer their prayers, and the Egyptians will be healed (CEV, Isaiah 19:22).

But to us, O Lord, be merciful, for we have waited for you. Be our strength each day and our salvation in times of trouble (TLB, Isaiah 33:2).

O Lord, by these things men live, and in all these things is the life of my spirit: so, wilt thou recover me, and make me to live. Behold, for peace I had great bitterness: but thou hast in love to my soul delivered it from the pit of corruption: for thou hast cast all my sins behind thy back (KJV, Isaiah 38:16-17).

He giveth power to the faint; and to them that have no might he increaseth strength (KJV, Isaiah 40:29).

Don't be afraid. I am with you. Don't tremble with fear. I am your God. I will make you strong, as I protect you with my arm and give you victories (CEV, Isaiah 41:10).

He suffered and endured great pain for us, but we thought his suffering was a punishment from God. He was wounded and crushed because of our sins; by taking our punishment, he made us completely well (CEV, Isaiah 53:4-5).

Why waste your money on what really isn't food? Why work hard for something that doesn't satisfy? Listen carefully to me, and you will enjoy the very best foods (CEV, Isaiah 55:2).

I know what you are like! But I will heal you, lead you, and give you comfort, until those who are mourning start singing my praises. No matter where you are. I, the Lord, will heal you and give you peace (CEV, Isaiah 57:18-19).

Then shall thy light break forth as the morning, and thine health shall spring forth speedily: and thy righteousness shall go before thee; the glory of the Lord shall be thy reward (KJV, Isaiah 58:8).

The Lord will always guide you and provide good things to eat when you are in the desert. He will make you healthy. You will be like a garden that has plenty of water or like a stream that never runs dry (CEV, Isaiah 58:11).

I will give you back your health again and heal your wounds. Now you are called "The Outcast" and "Jerusalem, the Place Nobody Wants" (TLB, Jeremiah 30:17).

Behold, [in the future restored Jerusalem] I will lay upon it health and healing, and I will cure them and will reveal to them the abundance of peace (prosperity, security, stability) and truth (AMP, Jeremiah 33:6).

Fruit trees will grow all along this river and produce fresh fruit every month. The leaves will never dry out, because they will always have water from the stream that flows from the temple, and they will be used for healing people (CEV, Ezekiel 47:12).

For the next ten days, let us have only vegetables and water at mealtime (CEV, Daniel 1:12).

The Rest of Nebuchadnezzar's Letter about His Second Dream

About twelve months later, I was walking on the flat roof of my royal palace and admiring the beautiful city of Babylon when these things started happening to me. I was saying to myself, "Just look at this wonderful capital city that I have built by my own power and for my own glory!" But before I could finish speaking, a voice from heaven interrupted: King Nebuchadnezzar, this kingdom is no longer yours. You will be forced to live with the wild animals, away from people. For seven years, you will eat grass, as though you were an ox, until you learn that God Most High is in control of all earthly kingdoms and that he is the one who chooses their rulers. This was no sooner said than done. I was forced to live like a wild animal; I ate grass and was unprotected from the dew. As time went by, my hair grew longer than eagle feathers, and my fingernails looked like the claws of a bird. Finally, I prayed to God in heaven, and my mind was healed. Then I said: "I praise and honor God Most High. God lives forever, and his kingdom will never end. To him, the nations are far less than nothing; God controls the stars in the sky and everyone on this earth. When God does something, we cannot change it or even ask why." At that time my mind was healed, and once again, I became the ruler of my glorious kingdom. My advisors and officials returned to me, and I had greater power than ever before.

That's why I say: "Praise and honor the King who rules from heaven! Everything he does is honest and fair, and he can shatter the power of those who are proud" (CEV, Daniel 4:28-37).

But unto you that fear my name shall the Sun of righteousness arise with healing in his wings, and ye shall go forth, and grow up as calves of the stall (KJV, Malachi 4:2).

Come and let us return to the Lord, for He has torn so that He may heal us; He has stricken so that He may bind us up (AMPC, Hosea 6:1).

Jesus went all over Galilee, teaching in their synagogues and preaching the good news about God's kingdom. He also healed every kind of disease and sickness. News about him spread all over Syria, and people with every kind of sickness or disease were brought to him. Some of them had a lot of demons in them, others were thought to be crazy, and still, others could not walk. But Jesus healed them all (CEV, Matthew 4:23-24).

Don't worry about tomorrow. It will take care of itself. You have enough to worry about today (CEV, Matthew 6:34).

Jesus heard them and answered, "Healthy people don't need a doctor, but sick people do" (CEV, Matthew 9:12).

And when he had called unto him his twelve disciples, he gave them power against unclean spirits, to cast them out, and to heal all manner of sickness and all manner of disease (KJV, Matthew 10:1).

Heal the sick, raise the dead to life, heal people who have leprosy, and force out demons. You received without paying, now give without being paid (CEV, Matthew 10:8).

"Are you tired? Worn out? Burned out on religion? Come to me. Get away with me and you'll recover your life. I'll show you how to take a real rest. Walk with me and work with me—watch how I do it. Learn the unforced rhythms of grace. I won't lay anything heavy or ill-fitting on you. Keep company with me and you'll learn to live freely and lightly" (MSG, Matthew 11:28-30).

Everyone was amazed at what they saw and heard. People who had never spoken could now speak. The lame were healed, the paralyzed could walk, and the blind were able to see. Everyone was praising the God of Israel (CEV, Matthew 15:31).

But Jesus beheld them, and said unto them, "With men this is impossible; but with God all things are possible" (KJV, Matthew 19:26).

Jesus answered: Love the Lord your God with all your heart, soul, and mind (CEV, Matthew 22:37).

Jesus Heals Many People

As soon as Jesus left the synagogue with James and John, they went home with Simon and Andrew. When they got there, Jesus was told that Simon's mother-in-law was sick in bed with fever. Jesus went to her. He took hold of her hand and helped her up. The fever left her, and she served them a meal. That evening after sunset, all who were sick or had demons in them were brought to Jesus. In fact, the whole town gathered around the door of the house. Jesus healed all kinds of terrible diseases and forced out a lot of demons. But the demons knew who he was, and he did not let them speak (CEV, Mark 1:29-34).

And besought him greatly, saying, my little daughter lieth at the point of death: I pray thee, come and lay thy hands on her, that she may be healed; and she shall live (KJV, Mark 5:23).

And he said unto her, Daughter, thy faith hath made thee whole; go in peace and be whole of thy plague (KJV, Mark 5:34).

Jesus said unto him, if thou canst believe, all things are possible to him that believeth (KJV, Mark 9:23).

You must love him with all your heart, soul, mind, and strength (CEV, Mark 12:30).

One day, some Pharisees and experts in the Law of Moses sat listening to Jesus teach. They had come from every village in Galilee and Judea and from Jerusalem. God had given Jesus the power to heal the sick, and some people came carrying a man on a mat because he could not walk. They tried to take him inside the house and put him in front of Jesus. But because of the crowd, they could not get him to Jesus. So they went up on the roof, where they removed some tiles and let the mat down in the middle of the room. When Jesus saw how much faith they had, he said to the man, "My friend, your sins are forgiven." The Pharisees and the experts began arguing, "Jesus must think he is God! Only God can forgive sins." Jesus knew what they were thinking, and he said, "Why are you thinking this? Is it easier for me to tell this man that his sins are forgiven or to tell him to get up and walk? But now you will see that the Son of Man has the right to forgive sins here on earth." Jesus then said to the man, "Get up! Pick up your mat and walk home" (CEV, Luke 5:17-24).

Jesus answered, "Healthy people don't need a doctor, but sick people do. I didn't come to invite good people to turn to God. I came to invite sinners" (CEV, Luke 5:31-32).

While Jesus was speaking, someone came from Jairus' home and said, "Your daughter has died! Why bother the teacher anymore?" When Jesus heard this, he told Jairus, "Don't worry! Have faith, and your daughter will get well." Jesus went into the house, but he did not let anyone else go with him, except Peter, John, James, and the girl's father and mother. Everyone was crying and weeping for the girl. But Jesus said, "The child isn't dead. She is just asleep." The people laughed at him because they knew she was dead. Jesus took hold of the girl's hand and said, "Child, get up!" She came back to life and got right up. Jesus told them to give her something to eat. Her parents were surprised, but Jesus ordered them not to tell anyone what had happened (CEV, Luke 8:49-56).

But when the crowds learned of it, [they] followed Him; and He welcomed them and talked to them about the kingdom of God and healed those who needed restoration to health (AMPC, Luke 9:11).

The man replied, "The Scriptures say, 'Love the Lord your God with all your heart, soul, strength, and mind.' They also say, 'Love your neighbors as much as you love yourself.'" (CEV, Luke 10:27).

And behold, there was a woman which had a spirit of infirmity eighteen years, and was bowed together, and could in no wise lift up herself. And when Jesus saw her, he called her to him, and said unto her, Woman, thou art loosed from thine infirmity. And he laid his hands on her: and immediately she was made straight, and glorified God (KJV, Luke 13:11-13).

Jesus Heals a Sick Man

One Sabbath, Jesus was having dinner in the home of an important Pharisee, and everyone was carefully watching Jesus. All of a sudden, a man with swollen legs stood up in front of him. Jesus turned and asked the Pharisees and the teachers of the Law of Moses, "Is it right to heal on the Sabbath?" But they did not say a word. Jesus took hold of the man. Then he healed him and sent him away. Afterwards, Jesus asked the people, "If your son or ox falls into a well, wouldn't you pull him out at once, even on the Sabbath?" There was nothing they could say (CEV, Luke 14:1-6).

A Warning

Don't spend all of your time thinking about eating or drinking or worrying about life. If you do, the final day will suddenly catch you (CEV, Luke 21:34).

You surely know that your body is a temple where the Holy Spirit lives. The Spirit is in you and is a gift from God. You are no longer your own. God paid a great price for you. So, use your body to honor God (CEV, 1 Corinthians 6:19-20).

When Jesus noticed him lying there [helpless], knowing that he had already been a long time in that condition, He said to him, Do you want to become well? [Are you really in earnest about getting well?] (AMPC, John 5:6).

Afterward, Jesus findeth him in the temple, and said unto him, Behold, thou art made whole: sin no more, lest a worse thing come unto thee (KJV, John 5:14).

"While I am in the world, I am the light for the world." After Jesus said this, he spit on the ground. He made some mud and smeared it on the man's eyes. Then he said, "Go wash off the mud in Siloam Pool." The man went and washed in Siloam, which means "One Who Is Sent." When he had washed off the mud, he could see. The man's neighbors and the people who had seen him begging wondered if he really could be the same man. Some of them said he was the same beggar, while others said he only looked like him. But he told them, "I am that man." "Then how can you see?" they asked. He answered, "Someone named Jesus made some mud and smeared it on my eyes. He told me to go and wash it off in Siloam Pool. When I did, I could see" (CEV, John 9:5-11).

The thief comes only in order to steal and kill and destroy. I came that they may have and enjoy life, and have it in abundance (to the full, till it overflows) (AMPC, John 10:10).

I give you peace, the kind of peace only I can give. It isn't like the peace this world can give. So don't be worried or afraid (CEV, John 14:27).

For the man to whom this sign (attesting miracle) of healing had happened was more than forty years old (AMP, Acts 4:22).

Show your mighty power, as we heal people and work miracles and wonders in the name of your holy Servant Jesus. After they had prayed, the meeting place shook. They were all filled with the Holy Spirit and bravely spoke God's message (CEV, Acts 4:30-31).

There he met a man named Aeneas, paralyzed and bedridden for eight years. Peter said to him, "Aeneas! Jesus Christ has healed you! Get up and make your bed." And he was healed instantly (TLB, Acts 9:33-34).

I'm sure you have heard about the Good News for the people of Israel—that there is peace with God through Jesus, the Messiah, who is Lord of all creation. This message has spread all through Judea, beginning with John the Baptist in Galilee. And you no doubt know that Jesus of Nazareth was anointed by God with the Holy Spirit and with power, and he went around doing good and healing all who were possessed by demons, for God was with him (TLB, Acts 10:37-38).

With dawn about to break, Paul called everyone together and

proposed breakfast: "This is the fourteenth day we've gone without food. None of us has felt like eating! But I urge you to eat something now. You'll need strength for the rescue ahead. You're going to come out of this without even a scratch!" (MSG, Acts 27:34).

As it happened, Publius's father was ill with fever and dysentery. Paul went in and prayed for him, and laying his hands on him, healed him (TLB, Acts 28:8).

Since these people refused even to think about God, he let their useless minds rule over them. That's why they do all sorts of indecent things (CEV, Romans 1:28).

Don't let sin rule your body. After all, your body is bound to die, so don't obey its desires, or let any part of it become a slave of evil. Give yourselves to God, as people who have been raised from death to life. Make every part of your body a slave that pleases God (CEV, Romans 6:12-13).

If our minds are ruled by our desires, we will die. But if our minds are ruled by the Spirit, we will have life and peace. Our desires fight against God because they do not and cannot obey God's laws (CEV, Romans 8:6-7).

We are assured and know that [God being a partner in their labor] all things work together and are [fitting into a plan] for good to and for those who love God and are called according to [His] design and purpose (AMPC, Romans 8:28).

Christ Brings New Life

Dear friends, God is good. So, I beg you to offer your bodies to him as a living sacrifice, pure and pleasing. That's the most sensible way to serve God. 2 Don't be like the people of this world, but let God change the way you think. Then you will know how to do everything that is good and pleasing to him (CEV, Romans 12:1-2).

Rejoicing in hope; patient in tribulation; continuing instant in prayer (KJV, Romans 12:12).

If any man defiles the temple of God, him shall God destroy; for the temple of God is holy, which temple ye are (KJV, 1 Corinthians 3:17).

What? know ye not that your body is the temple of the Holy Ghost, which is in you, which ye have of God, and ye are not your own? For ye are bought with a price: therefore, glorify God in your body, and in your spirit, which are God's (KJV, 1 Corinthians 6:19-20).

There hath no temptation taken you, but such as is common to man: but God is faithful, who will not suffer you to be tempted above that ye are able; but will with the temptation also make a way to escape, that ye may be able to bear it (KJV, 1 Corinthians 10:13).

When you eat or drink or do anything else, always do it to honor God (CEV, 1 Corinthians 10:31).

Let the Spirit change your way of thinking (CEV, Ephesians 4:23).

None of us hate our own bodies. We provide for them and take good care of them, just as Christ does for the church (CEV, Ephesians 5:29).

But the fruit of the Spirit is love, joy, peace, longsuffering, gentleness, goodness, faith, Meekness, temperance: against such there is no law (KJV, Galatians 5:22-23).

Be careful about nothing; but in everything by prayer and supplication with thanksgiving, let your requests be made known unto God. And the peace of God, which passeth all understanding, shall keep your hearts and minds through Christ Jesus (KJV, Philippians 4:6-7).

I can do all things through Christ which strengtheneth me (KJV, Philippians 4:13).

But my God shall supply all your need according to his riches in glory by Christ Jesus (KJV, Philippians 4:19).

God doesn't intend to punish us but wants us to be saved by our Lord Jesus Christ (CEV, 1 Thessalonians 5:9).

I pray that God, who gives peace, will make you completely holy. And may your spirit, soul, and body be kept healthy and faultless until our Lord Jesus Christ returns (CEV, 1 Thessalonians 5:23).

Don't waste time arguing over foolish ideas and silly myths and legends. Spend your time and energy in the exercise of keeping spiritually fit. Bodily exercise is all right, but spiritual exercise is much more important and is a tonic for all you do. So, exercise yourself spiritually, and practice being a better Christian because that will help you not only now in this life, but in the next life too (TLB, 1 Timothy 4:7-8).

Drink water no longer exclusively but use a little wine for the sake of your stomach and your frequent illnesses (AMPC, 1 Timothy 5:23).

For God hath not given us the spirit of fear, but of power, and of love, and of a sound mind (KJV, 2 Timothy 1:7).

For the grace of God (His unmerited favor and blessing) has come forward (appeared) for the deliverance from sin and the eternal salvation for all mankind (AMPC, Titus 2:11).

Is any sick among you? Let him call for the elders of the church; and let them pray over him, anointing him with oil in the name of the Lord: And the prayer of faith shall save the sick, and the Lord shall raise him up; and if he have committed sins, they shall be forgiven him (KJV, James 5:14-15).

Confess to one another therefore your faults (your slips, your false steps, your offenses, your sins) and pray [also] for one another, that you may be healed and restored [to a spiritual tone of mind and heart]. The earnest (heartfelt, continued) prayer of a righteous man makes tremendous power available [dynamic in its working] (AMPC, James 5:16).

Casting all your care upon him; for he careth for you (KJV, 1 Peter 5:7).

Who his own self bare our sins in his own body on the tree, that we, being dead to sins, should live unto righteousness: by whose stripes ye were healed (KJV, 1 Peter 2:24).

Don't forget that the Lord is patient because he wants people to be saved. This is also what our dear friend Paul said when he wrote you with the wisdom God had given him (CEV, 2 Peter 3:15).

He that loveth not knoweth not God; for God is love (KJV, 1 John 4:8).

Beloved, I wish above all things that thou mayest prosper and be in health, even as thy soul prospereth KJV, 3 John 2).

Then I heard a voice from heaven shout, "Our God has shown his saving power, and his kingdom has come! God's own Chosen One has shown his authority. Satan accused our people in the presence of God day and night. Now he has been thrown out!" (CEV, Revelation 12:10).

God's people must learn to endure. They must also obey his commands and have faith in Jesus (CEV, Revelation 14:12).

And God shall wipe away all tears from their eyes; and there shall be no more death, neither sorrow, nor crying, neither shall there be any more pain: for the former things are passed away (KJV, Revelation 21:4).

CHAPTER TEN

I AM With You

I AM the one that made the bush burn, and yet the bush was unharmed. I AM the one who was with Moses, Abraham, Isaac, and Jacob. I AM the maker and defender of the universe, the one true God: me and me alone, besides me there is no other. When you are hungry, I AM the bread of life, and when you are thirsty, I AM living water. When you are sick, I AM the greatest physician of all, the one willing to bind up all your wounds and heal your diseases. I AM the truth, the way, and the life. I knew you before you were conceived in your mother's womb. I knitted your bones and fashioned everything else together and wrapped them with flesh. I commanded you to take your first breath and welcomed you with open arms into the world. I watched you take your first step. I help you up when you fall. I AM with you when you lay down to sleep, and I AM with you when you rise in the morning. I will never leave you or forsake you. I AM with you always.

I AM.

This chapter deals with the three seasons of life; the prime of life, old age, and death as well as resurrection to life with God. My hope is that you will leave this chapter and this book with more confidence and faith in God and His wonderful plan for your life than ever before. So let these scriptures by evidence of God's preordained care for you be all the proof you need that God is with you.

Season One: Life

God is With You Because...

He has a plan for you

- You tried to harm me, but God made it turn out for the best so that he could save all these people, as he is now doing (CEV, Genesis 50:20).

He is with you

- I may walk through valleys as dark as death, but I won't be afraid. You are with me, and your shepherd's rod makes me feel safe (CEV, Psalms 23:4).

He promised to sustain you

- Our Lord, we belong to you. We tell you what worries us, and you won't let us fall (CEV, Psalms 55:22).

He can still whisper to storms

- Then they cried out to the Lord in their trouble (CEV, Psalms 107:6).
- You were in serious trouble, but you prayed to the Lord, and he rescued you (CEV, Psalms 107:13).

He is a God of mercy

- The Lord will perfect that which concerneth me; Thy mercy, O Lord, endureth forever; forsake not the works of Thine own hands (KJ21, Psalms 138:8).

He is holding your hand. He will help you.

- For I am the Lord your God who takes hold of your right hand and says to you, do not fear; I will help you (NIV, Isaiah 41:13).

He loves you

- The Lord your God wins victory after victory and is always with you. He celebrates and sings because of you, and he will refresh your life with his love" (CEV, Zephaniah 3:17).

The God that created Heaven and Earth values you

- Look at the birds in the sky! They don't plant or harvest. They don't even store grain in barns. Yet your Father in heaven takes care of them. Aren't you worth much more than birds? (CEV, Matthew 6:26).

With God, nothing is impossible.

- Jesus looked at them and said, "With man this is impossible, but with God all things are possible" (NIV, Matthew 19:26).
- Last, because no matter what you're going through, God promised to work all things for the Good of those that love Him (CEV, Romans 8:28).

Season Two: Old Age and Growing Old Gracefully
(All citations BSB)

In part, this verse reads: "Rise in the presence of the aged and honor the elderly face-to-face" (Leviticus 19:32). Do you need reassurance that you are still worthy of honor, even though you're older? The Bible gives it to you.

Honor your father and your mother, as the Lord your God has commanded you, so that you may live long and that it may go well with you in the land the Lord your God is giving you (Deuteronomy 5:16).

Not everyone becomes wise with age, but the book of Psalms says that those who number their days may "gain a heart of wisdom" (Psalms 90:12).

The godly are described as the cedars of Lebanon in the book of Psalms. "Even in old age, they will still produce fruit; they will remain vital and green. They will declare, 'The LORD is just! He is my rock! There is no evil in him!'" (Psalms 92:12-14).

Proverbs and Psalms are full of great verses about aging. This one state: "Gray hair is a crown of splendor; it is attained in the way of righteousness" (Proverbs 16:31).

What's another benefit of growing older? Grandchildren! This verse states: "Grandchildren are the crown of the aged" (Proverbs 17:6).

Your relationship with your parents may not be comfortable, but we are told in Proverbs that "If one curses his father or his mother, his lamp will be put out in utter darkness" (Proverbs 20:20).

Bible Verses About Embracing Aging

Not everyone faces each birthday with dread. Some are thankful for each year and embrace the idea of getting older. They look at their wrinkles and gray hairs as badges of honor.

Not everything about growing old is good. Proverbs' verse states that young men are stronger than old, but it reassures the elderly that "gray hair the splendor of the old" (Proverbs 20:29).

This verse reads: "Listen to your father who begot you and do not despise your mother when she is old" (Proverbs 23:22). In case you didn't know, begot is one of those fancy Bible words that means "bring into existence."

Those who are waiting for God's return are given this promise. The book of Isaiah states, "They'll soar on wings like eagles; they'll run and not grow weary; they'll walk and not grow tired" (Isaiah 40:31).

This verse reads: "And I will still be carrying you when you are old. Your hair will turn gray, and I will still carry you. I made you, and I will carry you to safety" (Isaiah 46:4). This verse offers a great deal of comfort to older adults. Who wouldn't like the idea of being "carried to safety" when your body is not working well?

It is usual for the body to break down as it ages. Regardless, we are given this promise in the book of 2 Corinthians: "Though outwardly we are wearing out, inwardly we are renewed day by day. Our suffering is light and temporary and is producing for us an eternal glory that is greater than anything we can imagine" (2 Corinthians 4:16-18)

It's sometimes hard being patient with people who aren't patient with you. If it were easy, we wouldn't have these reminders: "Do not rebuke an older man harshly" (1 Timothy 5:1).

If you are wavering about your responsibility to your family, here is what the Bible states: "But if anyone does not provide for his relatives, and especially for members of his household, he has denied the faith and is worse than an unbeliever" (1 Timothy 5:8).

It's not just men who are told to care for their mothers. "If any believing woman has relatives who are widows, let her care for them. Let the church not be burdened, so that it may care for those who are truly widows" (1 Timothy 5:16).

This verse from Titus is rather lengthy, but it can serve as a reminder of how older men and women are to act. "Older men are to be temperate, dignified, sensible, sound in faith, in love, in perseverance. Older women likewise are to be reverent in their behavior, not malicious gossips nor enslaved to much wine, teaching what is good, so that they may encourage the young women to love their husbands, to love their children, to be sensible, pure, workers at home, kind, being subject to their own husbands so that the word of God will not be dishonored" (Titus 2:2-5).

The Bible offers plenty of advice on how to live. This is found in the book of James: "Religion that is pure and undefiled before God, the Father, is this: to visit orphans and widows in their affliction and to keep oneself unstained from the world" (James 1:27).

Season Three: Death (Here today gone tomorrow or so it seems)

Bible Verses about Death

What does the Bible say about Death? What happens when we die according to the Word of God? We will all experience death in life and the loss of loved ones. Grief is a normal emotion, yet feels completely foreign as we experience it. The reality of loss reminds us of our mortality and the longing for more.

God has promised to be with us and to provide us with peace in the midst of pain. His word in the Bible also provides us with the comfort of eternal life in the kingdom of heaven for those who have faith in His Son, Jesus Christ. Below are collected Scriptures that can help you process the grief of death as well as Bible verses about life after death. Find peace and resolution in the love and divinity of God from the Bible.

A Prayer in the Midst of Death and Loss:
Our hearts are grieving with those who are hurting, for those who have lost loved ones, for those who have suffered such great tragedy at the hands of evil. We ask that you would be their Comforter, that you would cover them with your grace and mercy, surrounding them in peace during this dark time. Thank you, God, that you are surely with us. Thank you that you care, thank you that your Presence is close, and that you weep with those who weep. We need you. We know and believe beyond any doubt that your power and love will never fail.
Amen.

The Lord's Coming
My friends, we want you to understand how it will be for those followers who have already died. Then you won't grieve over them and be like people who don't have any hope. We believe

Jesus died and was raised to life. We also believe that when God brings Jesus back again, he will bring with him all who had faith in Jesus before they died. Our Lord Jesus told us that when he comes, we won't go up to meet him ahead of his followers who have already died. With a loud command and with the shout of the chief angel and a blast of God's trumpet, the Lord will return from heaven. Then, those who had faith in Christ before they died will be raised to life. Next, all of us who are still alive will be taken up into the clouds together with them to meet the Lord in the sky. From that time on, we will all be with the Lord forever. Encourage each other with these words (CEV, 1 Thessalonians 4:13-18).

Whether we live or die, it must be for the Lord. Alive or dead, we still belong to the Lord (CEV, Romans 14:8).

For if you live according to [the dictates of] the flesh, you will surely die. But if through the power of the [Holy] Spirit you are [habitually] putting to death (making extinct, deadening) the [evil] deeds prompted by the body, you shall [really and genuinely] live forever (AMPC, Romans 8:13).

For the wages of sin is death, but the gift of God is eternal life in Christ Jesus our Lord (NIV, Romans 6:23).

God will wipe away every tear from their eyes; and death shall be no more, neither shall there be anguish (sorrow and mourning) nor grief nor pain anymore, for the old conditions and the former order of things have passed away (AMP, Revelation 21:4).

and the dust returns to the ground it came from, and the spirit returns to God who gave it (NIV, Ecclesiastes 12:7).

Jesus replied, "I promise that today you will be with me in paradise" (CEV, Luke 23:43).

God loved the people of this world so much that he gave his only Son, so that everyone who has faith in him will have eternal life and never really die (CEV, John 3:16).

Jesus then said, "I am the one who raises the dead to life! Everyone who has faith in me will live, even if they die. And everyone who lives because of faith in me will never really die. Do you believe this?" (CEV, John 11:25-26).

The Message
   The Road
   "Don't let this rattle you. You trust God, don't you? Trust me. There is plenty of room for you in my Father's home. If that weren't so, would I have told you that I'm on my way to get a room ready for you? And if I'm on my way to get your room ready, I'll come back and get you so you can live where I live. And you already know the road I'm taking" (CEV, John 14:1-4).

For we believe that Jesus died and rose again, and so we believe that God will bring with Jesus those who have fallen asleep in him (NIV, 1 Thessalonians 4:14).

Listen, I tell you a mystery: We will not all sleep, but we will all be changed—in a flash, in the twinkling of an eye, at the last trumpet. For the trumpet will sound, the dead will be raised imperishable, and we will be changed. For the perishable must clothe itself with the imperishable, and the mortal with immortality. When the perishable has been clothed with the imperishable, and the mortal with immortality, then the saying that is written will come true: "Death has been swallowed up in victory." "Where, O death, is your victory? Where, O death, is your sting?" The sting of death is sin, and the power of sin is the law. But thanks be to God! He gives us the victory through our Lord Jesus Christ (NIV, 1 Corinthians

15:51-57).

And do not be afraid of those who kill the body but cannot kill the soul; but rather be afraid of Him who can destroy both soul and body in hell (Gehenna) (AMPC, Matthew 10:28).

Yes, though I walk through the [deep, sunless] valley of the shadow of death, I will fear or dread no evil, for You are with me; Your rod [to protect] and Your staff [to guide], they comfort me. You prepare a table before me in the presence of my enemies. You anoint my head with oil; my [brimming] cup runs over (AMPC, Psalms 23:4-5).

Once they die and are buried, that will be the end of all their plans. The Lord God of Jacob blesses everyone who trusts him and depends on him. God made heaven and earth; he created the sea and everything else. God always keeps his word (CEV, Psalms 146:4-6).

For the living know that they will die, but the dead know nothing; they have no further reward, and even their name is forgotten (NIV, Ecclesiastes 9:5).

Seize Life!
Still, anyone selected out for life has hope, for, as they say, "A living dog is better than a dead lion." The living at least know something, even if it's only that they're going to die. But the dead know nothing and get nothing. They're a minus that no one remembers. Their loves, their hates, yes, even their dreams, are long gone. There's not a trace of them left in the affairs of this earth (MSG, Ecclesiastes 9:5-6).

And just as it is appointed for [all] men once to die, and after that the [certain] judgment (AMP, Hebrews 9:27).

For I take no pleasure in the death of anyone, declares the Sovereign Lord. Repent and live! (NIV, Ezekiel 18:32).

If a man dies, shall he live again? All the days of my warfare and service, I will wait till my change and release shall come (AMP, Job 14:14).

That's why we live with such good cheer. You won't see us drooping our heads or dragging our feet! Cramped conditions here don't get us down. They only remind us of the spacious living conditions ahead. It's what we trust in but don't yet see that keeps us going. Do you suppose a few ruts in the road or rocks in the path are going to stop us?

When the time comes, we'll be plenty ready to exchange exile for homecoming (MSG, 2 Corinthians 5:6-8).

– MSG

The Death-Dealing Sin, the Life-Giving Gift

You know the story of how Adam landed us in the dilemma we're in—first sin, then death, and no one is exempt from either sin or death. That sin disturbed relations with God in everything and everyone, but the extent of the disturbance was not clear until God spelled it out in detail to Moses. So death, this huge abyss separating us from God, dominated the landscape from Adam to Moses. Even those who didn't sin precisely as Adam did by disobeying a specific command of God still had to experience this termination of life, this separation from God. But Adam, who got us into this, also points ahead to the One who will get us out of it (MSG, Romans 5:12-14).

Again, it is written.

The Lord's Coming

My friends, we want you to understand how it will be for those followers who have already died. Then you won't grieve over them and be like people who don't have any hope. We believe Jesus died and was raised to life. We also believe that when God brings Jesus back again, he will bring with him all who had faith in Jesus before they died. Our Lord Jesus told us that when he comes, we won't go up to meet him ahead of his followers who have already died. With a loud command and with the shout of the chief angel and a blast of God's trumpet, the Lord will return from heaven. Then, those who had faith in Christ before they died will be raised to life. Next, all of us who are still alive will be taken up into the clouds together with them to meet the Lord in the sky. From that time on, we will all be with the Lord forever. Encourage each other with these words (CEV, 1 Thessalonians 4:13-18).

May God Bless the reader, hearer, and doer of His Word.

For all citations, the following abbreviations were used throughout the text.

- AMP: Amplified Bible
- AMPC: Amplified Bible, Classic Edition
- BSB: English Berean Standard Version
- CEB: Common English Bible
- CEV: Contemporary English Version
- ESV: English Standard Version
- KJ21: 21st Century King James Version
- KJV: King James Version
- MSG: The Message
- NIV: New International Version
- NLT: New Living Translation
- TLB: The Living Bible

About the Author

The author, Stacey Baron Walker, was born on March 10, 1966. He is from St. Louis, MO, and currently resides in Gallatin, TN. From the moment he could sit in the adult church service, he has been fascinated with the Most-High God of heaven and earth and has sought to understand, communicate, and build a very intimate relationship with Him. Despite many challenges and adversities throughout his life, God has always been there and looked out for him. Stacey's heartfelt desire is that every person reached through his writing would receive the opportunity to know and experience God's breathtaking love and beneficial care in the same ways that he has.

9 798985 558159